ON NATURE'S TRAIL

ON NATURE'S TRAIL

An illustrated introduction to the sights and signs of the countryside

KEN HOY

MITCHELL
ARTISTS
HOUSE
BEAZLEY

Contents

Published in 1978 by Artists House,
Mitchell Beazley Marketing Limited,
Artists House, 14–15 Manette Street,
London W1V 5LB
Designed and produced for Artists House by
 Intercontinental Book Productions
Copyright © 1978 Intercontinental Book Productions

ISBN 0 86134 004 3 Printed in Italy

Introduction

Even if you live in the centre of a city the countryside is never far away – there are parks, allotments, wasteland and rivers, and the open fields and woods are usually less than an hour's travelling away. Yet we often give the countryside only a casual passing glance and are unaware of the diverse animal and plant life it contains. We overlook the exciting worlds that exist beneath the surface of a pond or in the leaf-litter of the forest floor.

You can easily learn to be observant and to see more than first meets the eye. When you know how to interpret the tracks and signs of animals you will understand more about their behaviour. It's easy, for instance, to distinguish between the tracks of foxes and dogs – dogs have blunter claws due to road-walking and, unlike the fox, do not have a thick tuft of hair growing underneath the foot; it may then surprise you to find how close foxes come to your home. And take a closer look at an oak tree next time you pass one; if you find hornbeam seeds wedged in the bark this shows – when you know – that a nuthatch has been feeding there.

The face of the countryside is constantly changing and different aspects of wildlife become more apparent at different times of the year. So this book is arranged in sections which broadly follow the seasonal changes from winter through to autumn and a corresponding interest in the countryside is created, and grows as the year advances. It opens with a section on the tracks and signs that creatures leave behind. (You'll find that bird and animal footprints are most easily seen in the snow and frosts of winter.) The following sections relate especially to spring, the season of new life and growth. At this time of year, the ponds are full of frogspawn, buds are swelling on previously bare branches and twigs,

mosses and lichens are prominent, and hedgerows and gardens are full of fledgling birds and caterpillars. Summer brings a profusion of flowers and insects, and, in autumn, the life of the woodlands is undergoing changes in preparation for winter.

Because the book develops along this seasonal cycle, you can explore the countryside and discover and observe its varied and interesting wildlife, no matter what the time of year or season. Just flick through the pages of this book and you will find useful information on almost anything new that catches your eye.

If you want to know more about the countryside, this is the guide you need – by following up its suggestions of what to look for you'll come across many new things. After dipping into it you'll be taking a closer and more thoughtful look at the next tree or bird you see. This book is about observation and discovery – the sort of discovery we all enjoy when we take a longer look and learn something new about what we thought we knew so well.

Far left: These frost crystals on a bramble are only one example of the numerous commonplace but beautiful sights which, whatever the season, can be enjoyed by anyone who stops to look.

Above left: There are intriguing sights for which there may not be an immediate answer – but a second, closer look may provide some clues. The foul smell of this fungus has attracted the flies to it. You will find out more about the stinkhorn and other fungi on page 48.

Below left: This picture shows a spot less than five miles from the centre of a city: there are bushes and trees, a stream, insects and birds, and innumerable small animals that live in the grass. Even in a city there are more intriguing places to explore than you might think.

Above right: Hiking or camping weekends and holidays can provide an ideal opportunity for the nature-lover to explore and study the countryside, and its diverse plant and animal life.

Right: You can probably reach the countryside in less than an hour's travelling. There you can find quiet corners like this, photographed on a lazy summer afternoon, where a fascinating web of life lies concealed among the grass, flowers and hedgerows. This picture was taken fourteen miles from the centre of London.

Tracks and Signs

Animal territory When you take a dog for a walk, he will almost certainly stop by a lamp-post or tree and will show great interest in sniffing it, checking to find out which other dogs have visited the spot. He will usually mark it with his own scent to let other dogs know that this is his walking territory.

When you see two robins or two blackbirds chase each other to and fro in a garden or park, they are establishing the boundaries between their territories – their feeding or breeding areas. First one is the pursuer, then the other. They rarely fight, as one or other will always give in first.

Many animals have regular pathways from which they stray only if they have a good reason. For example, a cat usually takes the same route across the flower beds and goes through the hedge or fence at the same place.

Such behaviour by dogs and cats and garden birds is familiar to the observant town dweller. It is not always so easy to observe similar events among the wild population of the countryside, but often signs are left behind which give clues of what has happened. Many people are familiar with the scratch marks left by a cat at its favourite stretching spot; badgers leave similar signs, often on elderberry shrubs which frequently grow around old setts. The badger and cat have another habit in common as both dig a hole into which they defecate. The badger, however, unlike the cat, does not fill the hole in afterwards. Foxes use not only urine to mark their territory but also faeces, which they usually deposit in a prominent place, such as on a mound or grass tussock. This behaviour is important in January and February when the scent which is added to the dropping is an indication to the opposite sex of readiness to mate. Rabbits also use droppings and urine to mark their territory. Rutting deer will also mark the ground with urine and scent from a gland below the eye.

Wild creatures often survive by habitual behaviour, thus, if it is safe on one occasion, it is likely to be so on another. Hence they often eat at the same places, travel on regular routes and cross ditches, roads, hedges and fences at regular spots.

Most animals see the world differently from humans. They see it as a network of safe pathways and highways between dangerous spots, a complexity of friendly, familiar smells and alarming scents where great caution must be observed. Other animals do not appear as hostile or friendly faces but as hostile or friendly smells.

In the countryside, smells tell animals what is happening and who is out and about. Humans do not have the same sense: they use their eyes rather than their noses.

Left: A nocturnal fox pauses – the scent of a field vole which crossed one of his own track-ways has attracted his attention. His nose tells him more than his eyes. Even in daylight his power of detecting scent takes priority over his eyesight.

Above: Foxes regularly mark their territory as they hunt. Marking is done not only *through the use of urine but also through droppings, or 'scats'. These are usually deposited in a prominent place such as a mound, stump or bank. The scat in the photograph has been placed on the top of a wood-ant nest. It is composed largely of fur and bone. In the summer scats are usually darker, as insects and berries account for part of the fox's diet at this time of year.*

Above: Signs of squirrel activity can be seen here. A dead tree that is devoid of bark will usually display evidence of this kind: the many scratches from the claws of squirrels indicate regular use. Just as hares, foxes and deer follow paths through the fields, so squirrels have equally well-worn routes through the trees. A squirrel that is released into a strange woodland will not know which branch to take to move from tree to tree. But a local squirrel will move across known routes along the branches as fast as one can walk over the ground below.

Right: This rabbit pathway, which has been well trodden out, is marked with droppings and the snow has also been stained with urine. This, too, is territorial behaviour.

Bottom: A network of rabbit roads criss-crossing in old sand dunes. On all such paths, the scent of previous footfalls will provide a certain security and familiarity for the rabbits.

Bird territory For the bird, too, the park or wood is an area where he feels safe and 'at home' and yet, just beyond the edge of the ground he knows so well, stretches place after place where he will feel frightened and cowardly. Back within his familiar territory he will be 'angry' and aggressive if another bird of his kind dares to enter; he will sing loudly and angrily to warn strangers to stay away.

This 'home territory' is something that all birds have to some degree. For some it is an area in the immediate vicinity of the nest, as in the case of rooks and gulls or other gregarious nesters. For others, like the larger predators, such as eagles, it may be several square miles. Most birds are aggressive about a 'territory' only in the breeding season but a few remain territorially aggressive – and thus sing – all the year. The European robin, of the snowy Christmas card, is by no means a bearer of tidings of good will and joy. On the contrary, his is the classic example of this aggressive behaviour, as he allows no other robin into his territory – not even his own mate, except in the spring when boundaries are redrawn and the two share a common area.

In the case of most of the common garden birds, the males begin to take up a territory as spring approaches and they stake their claim to it by singing – mainly to warn off intruding males rather than to attract females. Singing in the territory will continue until the end of the breeding season. Apart from providing a 'personal' feeding area, territory is important in another sense. Competition for nest sites in some species is fierce and birds that nest in holes can be particularly vulnerable. Shortage of sites certainly occurs when large numbers of trees are lost in such circumstances as the rapid spread of the Dutch Elm disease, and consequently, owls and birds of prey may be forced to leave an area.

Holes in trees often carry clues that identify the inhabitants. An area of ground at the foot of a tree and covered with wood chippings will indicate recent excavations of a nest hole by woodpeckers. If the hole is clean and round, the woodpeckers may well be in occupation. If, however, the entrance is marked by droppings then starlings who usually dirty their doorstep have taken over. Gnawed edges and a dirt-smudged entrance will show the presence of the grey squirrel. A house martin's mud nest with dry grass hanging from the entrance has been commandeered by house sparrows, but, on completion, the entrance will be too narrow for sparrows.

Left: Owls nest in large holes in trees which they use for roosting during the day-time. Tawny owls sometimes roost close against the trunk and are occasionally discovered by blackbirds, jays and tits whose scolding alarm cries are useful in detecting an owl's whereabouts.

Below: This photograph shows a young grey squirrel. These squirrels were introduced into the British Isles from the United States in the nineteenth century and can now be found in most of the deciduous woodlands in Britain. They are not found elsewhere in Europe.

Above: This juvenile house martin was fed for the first two weeks of its life in a nest where the narrow oval entrance was hardly wide enough for more than two young heads to poke out at the same time. If it survives the flight to and from South Africa as soon as the chill days of autumn arrive, it will return by the following May to the eaves under the same house which was imprinted on its mind as a young fledgling. If one wishes to prevent house sparrows from occupying the nests before the martins return, it is always advisable to destroy enough of the nest to render it useless for the sparrows. The martins will rebuild the mud nest when they arrive, by which time the house sparrows will be nesting elsewhere.

Below left: The nuthatch uses mud or clay to secure the nest site against would-be evictors. A hole or crack in a tree is selected and the entrance is then reduced to 3–4 cm (1–1·5 in) by plastering mud around the entrance. In the photograph, a crack in an oak has been filled in with clay above and below the desired entrance, to make the cavity more suitable.

Below right: A hole in a crab apple tree originally excavated by a pair of great spotted woodpeckers. A pair of starlings drove the woodpeckers away and reared a brood of young there. The following winter, grey squirrels gnawed the edges of the hole, enlarging it sufficiently to enable them to enter. No starlings or woodpeckers used it the following spring!

Tale telling signs   The drawing below is taken from a sketch in a naturalist's notebook made on a snowy, darkening, January afternoon – it tells of a drama that probably occurred the previous night. Look at the drawing and think about it before reading the 'Notebook' with the notes that accompanied the original sketch.

Notebook   Jan. 3rd. Temperature below freezing – snow-covered ground. Followed stoat tracks – found spot where it had waited behind a tree root – the snow slightly melted there. Beyond the tree root was a wood mouse hole in the snow-covered brambles. The mouse's tracks led from the hole to an area of disturbed snow where they met the stoat's tracks. The snow was speckled with spots of blood and a few wood mouse hairs where the stoat had captured and killed it. The stoat tracks led away for 200 yds (180 metres), and disappeared under the roots of a fallen tree. On the right-hand side of each set of tracks were the marks left by the hindfeet and tail of the mouse as the stoat carried it away.

The harsh drama of a bitter night is not always so easily interpreted and the story told by the trails and signs is not always so dramatic.

Snow provides conditions in which it is possible to find out more in a few hours about the wild life of an area, than days and weeks of searching will provide in the summer. Tracks are obvious and reveal not only the presence of an animal but its movements, habits and methods of hunting. Other signs often accompany the tracks and the snow makes them visible – the remains of nuts, seeds and other feeding signs, blood, fur and feathers. Holes, homes and regular pathways also become apparent as well as the interpretation of a sequence of events, for example, when fox tracks leading from an earth stop, showing all four feet and a circle on the snow of dead leaves, sand and soil where the fox has shaken itself.

The marks on the trees on the opposite page also provide information and facts which tell us something of earlier events. You need to be observant to notice them and thoughtful to interpret them.

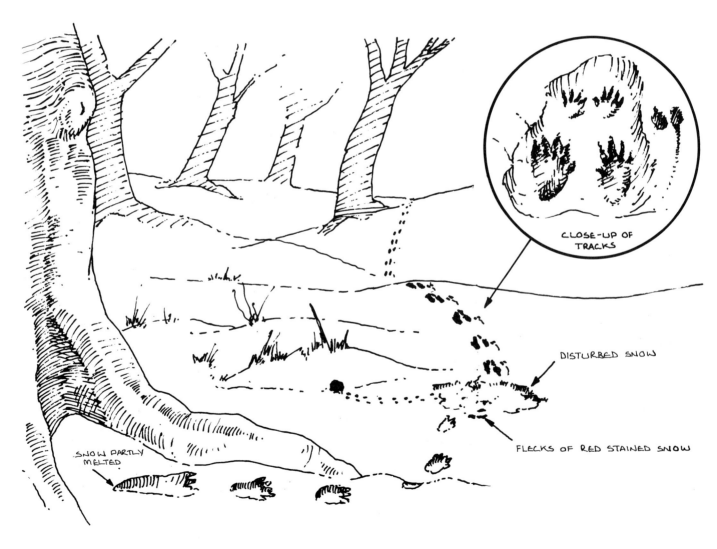

CLOSE-UP OF TRACKS

DISTURBED SNOW

SNOW PARTLY MELTED

FLECKS OF RED STAINED SNOW

Above: Another gruesome tale: whether a traffic casualty or a victim of the stoat whose tracks were nearby, this blackbird has helped to keep alive other creatures during a period of frost and snow. A small hole bitten in the skull points to the stoat. Crows, jays or magpies were not involved – they would have pulled the skeleton apart. Starlings, tits and even shrews or mice may well have taken part in the final scavenging as the skeleton has been picked clean so delicately.

Upper left: Damage to hedge growth and to trees can be devastating when horses are turned out without adequate fencing or sufficient grass. A favourite bark is the elm – as in this photograph, where the field was over-grazed and an elm sapling used as a fence post. If the large teeth marks did not tell us, the height of the damage clears rabbits and hares from any blame.

Upper right: Permanent damage has been caused in this young apple orchard by hares and rabbits during a spell of frost and snow. For such vegetarian animals, bark is the natural winter feed when the ground is covered and green vegetation unobtainable. Plastic tubing is often used around fruit trees to provide protection from damage such as is shown here.

Below left: Bark stripping in this case is by a different creature with a different objective. This young oak, killed by fire, has had the bark stripped and shredded by a grey squirrel who required a lining for its drey or nest. The inner bark, or bast, is a favourite material for this purpose. The squirrel ran off before the camera was close enough to photograph it. However, had it not been seen, the teeth marks alone would have provided sufficient clues to eliminate birds as gatherers of the bark for nest material.

Below right: The teeth marks and their position on this holly bark, leaves and twigs, suggest a larger animal than hares or rabbits who would have stripped the lower bark as well. A search of the ground for tracks confirms the presence of fallow deer. Deer, like other ruminants, have front teeth in the lower jaw only. The upper jaw has a horny pad against which the lower incisors act. In frosty weather, rabbits and hares will eat holly, but the signs then are leaves snipped off and lying on the ground and the remaining twig neatly cut.

The presence of animals and birds can often be detected by the signs of feeding activities: these may be teethmarks or the debris left behind. Like tracks, signs of debris are very temporary, either rotting, blowing away or disappearing with the first rain. Teeth marks and gnawing remain visible for longer – sometimes for years, when the damage to trees can be permanent and the timber as such ruined by the consequent irregular growth. Some tracks, droppings and teeth marks have achieved great fame by becoming fossils!

Sometimes, in extreme weather conditions when snow covers the ground for weeks, it is only by the signs left on the snow that it is possible to tell how some creatures survive. On one such occasion, groups of bullfinches were some of the few birds remaining deep in the forest. They survived by eating the dried blackberries that remained on bramble sprays left over from the autumn – the husks of the seeds lying on the surface of the snow told the story. Chaffinches also survived, as their tracks under birch trees showed, by eating the fallen birch seeds dropped by tits, goldfinches, redpolls and siskins feeding in the trees above. In such conditions, ducks had disappeared from the frozen lakes but their webbed footprints showed where they had rummaged beneath the snow under oak trees for acorns. Fallow deer had churned the leaves beneath sweet chestnut, crab apple, and oak trees – the nuts and fruit being their objective. Considerable damage is done to trees where there is frost or snow. Not only deer, but hares, rabbits, squirrels, voles and mice will eat the bark of trees. Both squirrels and jays will burrow and poke into the snow to find buried nuts and seeds and although both spend a lot of time in the autumn burying such fruits as acorns, it is very doubtful whether those that bury are the same individuals that 'remember' and dig the store out. Squirrels could probably locate such food by scent but how a jay can 'find' it is difficult to explain as birds have little or no sense of smell.

Sometimes the signs are very small and a trained eye is required to notice their significance. Often, commonly observed events are mistakenly dismissed as common knowledge. An obvious clue to an animal's presence is the hair caught in a wire fence. Often it is from a fox or badger or even a deer – for deer will prefer to crawl under a fence if they can. Always look around for tracks nearby. The clue may, of course, be from a domestic animal.

A lot of mystery still surrounds the everyday lives of many common creatures and careful observations can sometimes be of considerable value. The seasonal variation of some species' diets is often not fully appreciated and strange behaviour may sometimes defy explanation. For example, an answer has been found only recently to explain the hedgehog's habit of anointing itself with saliva. This is done, it seems, after biting on the poisonous skin of a toad. It is this that makes the sharp prickles of the hedgehog poisonously painful.

Left: Perhaps the classic sign of animal activity is the stump left when a beaver has been at work. The evidence often remains visible for several years. Stumps like this one are now only found in parts of North America and in a few forests in northern Europe and the lower Rhône, but the beaver was once widespread across Europe, including Britain, and may have played a larger part in changing the scenery than any other single animal.

Above: The photograph shows an oak with hundreds of hornbeam seeds wedged in the cracks of its bark. This is characteristic behaviour of the nuthatch, a bird whose name derives from 'nuthacker', for the seed can be more easily split and the kernel extracted when so wedged in a tree trunk. The nuthatch usually lives in woodlands and feeds on insects, spiders, nuts and seeds. Its bill is slender and pointed.

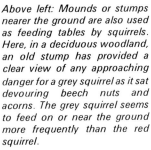

Above left: Mounds or stumps nearer the ground are also used as feeding tables by squirrels. Here, in a deciduous woodland, an old stump has provided a clear view of any approaching danger for a grey squirrel as it sat devouring beech nuts and acorns. The grey squirrel seems to feed on or near the ground more frequently than the red squirrel.

Top right: The photograph shows a bank vole's 'dining-room' under a log in September; at this time of year its diet will be largely made up of seeds. This vole has had a feast of black-berries, some rose hip seeds, and buttercup and grass seeds; it seems not to like the unripe seeds of the blackberry. Earlier, during the summer months, the remains of insects and even banded snails could probably be found.

Centre right: As this picture of a feeding area under a fallen tree trunk shows, seeds such as these hornbeam seeds are frequently gnawed by wood-

mice and bank voles. When the seeds are neatly split in two halves it is usually correctly claimed that it is the work of birds such as greenfinches, chaffinches, and hawfinches. However, mice or voles some-times do this as split seeds can be found in places where the small mammals have been feed-ing and where it is impossible for birds to feed, such as hollows under logs. Split seeds are pre-sent in this photograph. Per-sonal observation may be ac-curate but generalizations are best made with caution as ex-ceptions can often be found.

Bottom right: Squirrels' 'left-overs' are one of the commonest signs to be found in woodland. In coniferous woods, stripped cones – usually the work of red squirrels which are quite rare in Britain now – are a common sight. The scales are gnawed off to get to the small seeds which form a major item of diet. Some-times, when the feeding takes place on a favourite branch, the ground beneath is littered with cones and scales.

Tracks The tracks of most animals form a recognizable pattern. However, the pattern will change according to conditions and whether the animal bounds or hops instead of walking or running.

Tracks are most noticeable in snow but they can be found on muddy paths or on the mud and silt of drying ponds, lakes and rivers – especially after floods have subsided – or in tidal conditions. Tracks can also be seen in sand, and in dust and soot in buildings.

Tracks in snow are best recorded with a notebook and a black pencil or with a camera. A ruler is important to take measurements. Sometimes it is possible to say whether the tracks are hare, rabbit or stoat, merely by the size of the signs left.

Tracks on a muddy path or in the sandy silt beside a stream are best recorded by making a plaster cast of the markings.

Top: The tracks of chaffinches shown here under birch trees illustrate another form of scavenging for food, for in severe weather nothing can go to waste. Up above in the birch twigs, siskins, lesser redpolls and blue tits have hung on the ends of the twigs taking seeds from the birch catkins. Many seeds have been shaken on to the snow – enough to interest the chaffinches.

Above centre: The two sets of squirrel tracks illustrated in this photograph were made at different times when the condition of the snow had changed. The deep prints on the left were made when the snow was fresh and soft. The finer footprints on the right were made after three changes of conditions: the surface had thawed, re-frozen and had been dusted with a light fall of fine, new, powdery snow – ideal conditions for showing up this second set of tracks.

Left: The squirrel that made these tracks was trying hard to cope with very difficult circum-stances. The snow was 20–23 cm (8–9 in) deep and the squirrel could not leap clear of the snow with each bound – thus the result was the unusual pattern shown here. However, the squirrel's tail could not clear the snow completely and the groove it made shows clearly between the tracks.

Top right: This photograph shows a very clear set of wing prints which was made when a pheasant took off with a whirr of wings at the edge of a country lane. The result is an attractively symmetrical pattern in the snow.

Bottom right: Ideal snow conditions produced almost perfect prints of the forefeet of a fox. He paused under a bush to scent the air of a rabbit burrow, stepped forward and sniffed again. The needle points of his claws have just pricked the snow. These sharp claw marks are a useful identification point in distinguishing between fox and dog prints. Remember a dog's claws are nearly always blunted by walking on floors and roads.

16

To make a plaster cast

This is what is needed: Plaster of Paris from the chemist (best kept in a plastic bag in a tin); a small bowl or basin (plastic is lighter to carry); an old tablespoon; several strips of flexible card of appropriate sizes; some paper clips; several old newspapers; a trowel; (water is heavy and you can usually find plenty in a stream or ditch).

1 Having decided which is the best track, bend a strip of card into a ring and fasten it with a paper clip.
2 Press the cardboard ring firmly into the mud around the track.
3 Spoon the plaster into a suitable amount of water in the bowl and leave for a few moments. Then stir – the mixture should be like thick cream.
4 Pour the mixture carefully into the cardboard mould and *leave it*.
5 After ten to fifteen minutes carefully dig up the cast, together with plenty of mud to avoid breaking the plaster.
6 Then wrap it up in newspaper and put it in your rucksack.
7 Scratch the date and place on the back or top of the cast when hardened.
8 *Try to leave it alone for 24 hours!!* – before gently brushing away the mud under water.

You will have a mould of the foot and the surrounding mud. To reproduce the footprint at any time, you can press the plaster cast into soft mud or silty sand, or make a 'positive' of your 'negative' mould by repeating the whole process. To prevent the two casts bonding together first smear the negative cast lightly with vaseline.

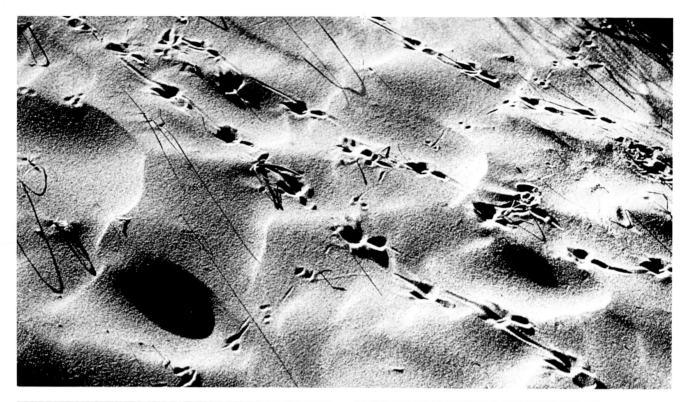

Top: Tracks in sand-dunes show up especially well in the very early morning after a heavy dew has damped the surface of the sand. The picture here shows three sets of scavenging crow tracks moving from right to top left. The crow's claws have just scored the sand between each footprint. The small tracks which cross the crow tracks to the bottom left of the picture are those of a woodmouse. The tail mark between the tracks can be seen clearly in the early morning sunshine.

Above centre: The young wood-mouse pictured here was discovered by following his tracks. A little bedraggled by the early morning dew, he was surprised in the open sand. In such an unfamiliar habitat there was no-where for him to hide, so instead he 'froze' and pretended not to be there!

Left: A common seal basked in the sun on this sandbank as the tide receded. The sea had with-drawn further when the seal was disturbed by human beings and needed to seek the safety of the water. The slithering of its body shows in the centre of the tracks. The cavities on either side are caused by the flippers as the seal levered its body down the slope. The claws on the flippers scored the sand at the end of each stroke made.

The tracks of the rabbit are familiar to most people who have walked in a snow-covered landscape. The basic pattern is often similar in many animals – rabbits, hares, mice and squirrels – the two hindfeet are opposite each other and more widely set than the two forefeet which, in the pattern, appear *behind* the hindfeet.

In the case of rabbit and hare tracks, as the gentle hop speeds up and becomes a galloping run, so the position of the forefeet changes the pattern.

The fixed pattern of an animal trail in the snow can give a false impression of how it came to be formed. It represents the points at which an animal touched the surface while in the process of continuous movement. Although the tracks may appear to be in groups, the four feet are unlikely to be on the ground at the same moment.

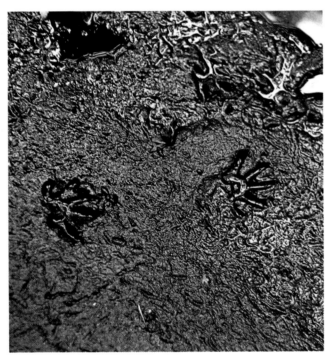

Above: In the mud beside an Illinois river, a raccoon left these clear, widely spread prints of its forefeet. No doubt it was looking for fish – one of its favourite foods. A native of North America, the raccoon has escaped from captivity and occurs in a feral state in one or two parts of northern Europe.

Far right: These rabbit tracks in the snow show the pattern common to many tracks; that is, the larger hindfeet tracks beside each other, while the forefeet are one behind the other. At the bottom of the picture the rabbit sat down on his haunches with his forefeet close together – then he moved away with steady bounding hops. The tracks are shown again in the diagram. Beside them, the shaded area represents the rabbit's body, linking hind- and forefeet – with the hindfeet on the ground and forefeet about to land. As the forefeet land the hindfeet come up past them to begin the next set of tracks. As the speed of the bounding hops increases to a run, the position of the forefeet moves until they are almost behind each other and thus the pattern changes at the top of the diagram. The photograph, on the far right, also shows this pattern. Hare and rabbit tracks are very similar – the larger size of the hare being the main difference between them.

The 'grass-roots' world

Tracks and signs of the smaller mammals – the mice, voles and shrews – are not always easy to find but their activity can be concentrated and observed more easily by creating a safe habitat to which they are attracted. Sheets of metal, old doors and other coverings placed in waste land and undisturbed corners will be used by these small mammals in many ways. After a few weeks, runs will be found criss-crossing the area, nests and sleeping quarters will be formed and small feeding cavities will contain the remains of food. Many other creatures will take advantage of this.

As the grass and vegetation under the cover dies, the conditions there begin to approximate to those at the bottom of an area of tall grass or herbage. There is an important exception which applies especially to metal sheets – that is, they react quickly to temperature change. Thus, in frosty or hot, sunny weather the area beneath them is uninhabitable by most creatures, owing to the icy cold or intense heat – although ants seem to like the warm, dry conditions. If the sheet is not lifted too often, lizards, slow worms and grass snakes may be found. Frogs, toads or newts appear in the autumn and spring, no doubt taking temporary shelter; bees, wasps and ants build nests there and beetles, spiders, slugs and snails find shelter during the daytime. In short, such a device provides a convenient opportunity for the naturalist to take the top off the world below the grass and observe the creatures that inhabit the grass-roots.

Creatures that live in the world of the grass-roots have enemies among themselves; for instance, a frog eats a beetle, but is itself eaten, in turn, by a grass snake. Mice and voles, who live on a diet of insects, need to watch out for stoats, weasels and foxes. However, some of the main predators of the grasslands descend from above. The kestrels and owls feed largely on mice and voles. Such small animals have extremely rapid rates of reproducing themselves, especially in favourable conditions which, on rare occasions, have produced local plagues – usually of the field vole. When this has occurred it has been noticeable how quickly the population of bird predators has increased, significantly controlling the spread of voles.

Pellets

One of the reasons why we know more about the food of birds of prey and owls is the fact that they conveniently provide us with clues after each meal. Indigestible items in their food, such as bones, fur, feathers and insect remains, are regurgitated a few hours after every meal. These can be found in large cavities in trees where owls roost or underneath the tree. Regurgitated pellets can sometimes be found below isolated trees, hedgerows, and posts and poles in marshland.

Opposite page, top: The hair on the underneath of the foot shows well on the forepaw of this dead fox — domesticated dogs do not have such a large tuft of hair growing between their toes. The fox, like several other animals, has strong scent pores in the pads of its feet, thus it can mark the ground with scent as it walks.

Opposite page, bottom: A fox print is not always easy to distinguish from a dog print of similar size except that a dog usually has extremely blunt claws — the result of road-walking. In the photograph, not only can the distinctive sharp claw marks of the fox be seen but, faintly showing in the centre of the print, there are also the marks made by the thick tuft of hair that grows underneath the fox's foot. No doubt this is of value to the fox in walking and hunting silently. When walking normally, a fox places his feet down in a straight line and usually the hindfeet register in the prints left by the forefeet.

Above: Under a sheet of corrugated metal a field vole reared a family. During the following winter, other voles, probably of the same family, continued using the area. They fed there in safety — this was shown by the piles of seed husks, small pieces of grass and broken, banded snail shells which littered the feeding spots. They also used the old nest of dried, shredded grass. The following spring, however, a queen bumble bee, that had passed the winter in hibernation, took over the voles' nest of shredded grass and beneath it began to construct the first wax cells of what was to become a new colony. The photograph above was taken in July and the dry grass has been parted to show the cells. The metal sheet, however, was in partial shade and therefore did not receive too much sun.

Right: Bird tracks are often found in the mud of estuaries, beside rivers and streams, and in ditches. The particularly clear tracks pictured here occurred when a moorhen walked down a polluted ditch. In size they are almost as large and just as broad as those of the pheasant. The moorhen, however, has a long hind toe which hardly shows at all in pheasant tracks.

21

By soaking a pellet in water the remains of the prey can sometimes be identified. Fur and feathers can be separately recognized under a microscope. The average country walker can discover quite a lot, however, using a 10 × lens. There are a few simple, easily recognized criteria which help:

1 Pellets containing numbers of complete bones are nearly always from owls. Pellets without bone or only small, part-digested pieces are usually from birds of prey.

2 The pellet's length varies with the contents but the diameter can indicate the bird's size.

3 The skulls of shrews and moles (insectivores) differ from those of mice and voles (rodents). The teeth of the former are in a continuous row along either side of the long, rather flattened skull. However, mice and voles have long front (incisor) teeth separated from the back teeth (molars) by a considerable gap.

4 Voles' teeth are quite different from those of mice. The three cheek teeth, or molars, fit into one long socket in the jaw and the teeth are ridged longitudinally on either side, whereas the teeth of mice have separate roots, each with its own jaw socket.

5 The wood mouse can be distinguished from the house mouse by the number of roots and sockets present in the front upper molar. The house mouse's tooth has a three-pronged root, while the wood mouse has four – the harvest mouse has five.

Sadly, the above information is also valuable in identifying mammal remains found in carelessly discarded bottles in ditches, hedgerows, undergrowth, wasteland, lay-bys and the roadside. Bottles titled upwards are easily entered because the hind-feet are in contact with the ground. Care in the disposal of picnic rubbish is not only desirable for the preservation of our countryside but, as we can see, it also helps to preserve our wildlife.

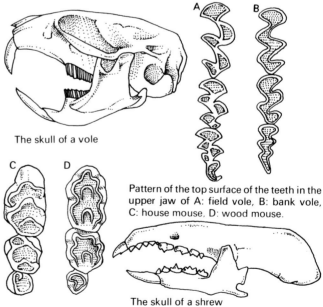

The skull of a vole

Pattern of the top surface of the teeth in the upper jaw of A: field vole, B: bank vole, C: house mouse, D: wood mouse.

The skull of a shrew

Top: This field vole constructed a new nest in a corner of a covered area and reared a family there. In the photograph it is eating in a feeding hollow – a vegetarian, unlike the shrew, its staple food is grass and sedges. Field voles can be found in woods, fields and gardens.

Left: This pellet was found in open woodland in early August. As the pellet consists largely of insect remains it was probably produced by a young, inexperienced, night-flying tawny owl who was not sufficiently skilled to catch anything but beetles and moths, and perhaps worms.

Above left: A little owl's pellet, found in the winter time and containing field vole fur and bones. The front of the vole's skull and two orange-coloured front teeth, together with one of the lower jaw bones, are clearly visible in the pellet.

Above right: Beneath an elm tree, pellets cast up by little owls could be found throughout the year – indicating that the tree was used for roosting. These two pellets contain mice and vole bones and fur, and pieces of violet-black wing-cases of

beetles. Up to ninety per cent of the little owl's diet consists of invertebrates.

Below: A discarded bottle trapped a field vole – although it could get in it could not escape. The bottle contained water, as

the algae show, and this would have made the glass very slippery. Sometimes the presence of one victim attracts others, so that some bottles have been found to contain several skeletons of small creatures – sometimes thirty or more.

Birds

Birds have proved themselves extremely versatile in adapting to their environment. From the manner of their birth to the ways in which they obtain their food, their specialist features are determined by their need to survive. Diet, feet, beaks, bills, feathers, wing shape and colouring all contribute.

Growing up Human beings have longer lives than most other creatures and their rate of development is comparatively slow, so we wonder sometimes at the speed of change and of growth in other forms of life. In July the caterpillar of the peacock butterfly pupates, becomes a chrysalis and, within three weeks, the 'pulp' and liquids within the caterpillar have become a butterfly. Birds change almost as fast at the beginning of their lives. Within twelve days a starling's completed clutch of eggs will hatch. Twenty days later, five grey-clad and squawking youngsters leave the nest.

The rate at which young birds grow varies considerably. Those that are reared in the safety of a well-made and concealed nest are usually naked and blind when hatched from the egg; some, such as owls and birds of prey can take a long time developing before becoming fully fledged. Ground-nesting birds – such as snipe, woodcock and wading birds, ducks, gulls and terns, pheasants, partridges and grouse – all develop to a stage where they are insulated from cold with a coating of down, and are sufficiently active to be able to run and hide within a few hours of hatching. Herons are even more specialized – usually four of their eggs hatch at well-spaced intervals.

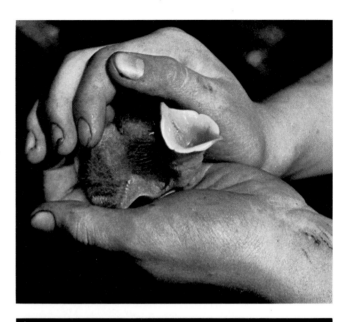

Above: This sixteen-day-old chicken embryo shows an incredible rate of growth. It is already three-quarters of the way through its incubation period.

Top right: Starling four to five days after hatching.

Centre right: After fourteen days.

Bottom right: Twenty days later.

24

Above left: In ground-nesting species of birds, where the dangers are greater, the change is even more rapid: the young are *clothed in down and grow to an active stage before hatching. This is a mallard duck's nest at 9 a.m. on the 28th day.*

Above right: By 10.15 a.m. this was happening – the chicks were hatching as pictured here. At midday the nest was empty *and the family were already on their way to a lake over half a mile away. Most of them reached it safely!*

Did you know that . . .

A bird's heartbeat is much faster than that of a human, which is about 70 beats per minute. In the crow family the heartbeat is relatively slow at about 350 beats. Most small birds have a heartbeat of about 500 to 600 but the North American hummingbird ticks over at a steady 1,000 beats per minute.

Fifteen to twenty per cent of the body weight of many birds is accounted for by the pair of massive pectoral muscles that power their wings. In strong fliers, like pigeons, this is as much as a third of their total weight. When cooked, this is the 'breast meat'.

The ruby-throated hummingbird of North America has one of the fastest re-corded wing-beats at 75 times per second.

The Californian condor, of which there are only a handful of breeding pairs left, has one of the largest wing spans at 2·7 m (9 ft).

The feathers of most birds weigh more than their skeleton. In the case of birds of prey, the feathers weigh twice as much.

Owls have one ear lower than the other. This exaggerates the slight difference in time between one ear and the other when hearing the same sound, thus improving the bird's ability to locate the source of the sound – an advantage in the dark.

A tawny owl can rotate its head through a full 360 degrees. Like most predators, it has good binocular vision in front – necessary to chase and catch its prey. But to see behind, when hunting from a perched position, it needs to turn its head.

Birds, like the buzzard, which are able to see fine detail at a great distance, have five times more rods and cones in their eyes than do humans.

Birds have three 'eyelids'. The third membrane is transparent so that the eye can be wiped without interrupting vision.

A woodcock has slightly better bino-cular vision behind than it has in front. When its beak is probing in deep mud, eyes on the sides of its head giving good 'rear' (above) vision are an essential for survival.

Above: Sometimes animal remains are apparent in droppings. These are green woodpecker droppings, which are often to be found on ant hills. The woodpecker's powerful beak can break open the ant hill, and

its long sticky tongue can penetrate deep into the tunnels of the ants' nest. The woodpecker droppings contain the outer skeletons of the ants, which are a major source of food for the birds.

Below left: The woodpecker's long tongue is wrapped inside its head and can winkle out insects from behind the bark.

Above: This photograph is of a rather abnormal pellet which

was produced by a jackdaw that was found with a broken wing. The snail diet may have resulted from the jackdaw's inability to fly, which meant that it needed to search the ground vegetation for sources of food.

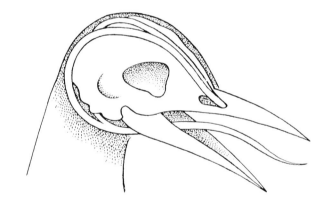

Diet and digestion Once launched into the world, birds are highly adapted to their environment, in particular with regard to their feeding. Their survival depends on the availability of food. The pellets which some birds cough up are one example of this adaptation.

Owls are not the only birds that eject pellets of indigestible food. Birds of prey, and members of the crow and gull families all do so. Fish-eating birds produce pellets of bones. Many other birds, whose food consists not only of plants but also of animals, will at times need to rid their digestive systems of hard material such as bones, scales, fur, feather quills and the shells and body casings of invertebrates that have accumulated in their gizzards.

Generally the diameter of the pellet is an indication of the size of the bird, whereas the shape varies with the species. Most frequently, pellets are found under roosting perches or, in the case of gulls

and wading birds, on the sandbanks or mudflats where the birds have been resting between periods of feeding.

Pellets can sometimes be confused with droppings but the latter are not so large. Both provide us with information about the bird's food, and both can be found more often than might be supposed once you start to look for them.

Many seeds have a tough covering which, if they are swallowed whole, resist the bird's digestive acids. This, of course, favours the plant and enables the seed to be more widely distributed after passing through the bird. Thus, seeds may frequently be found in the droppings of birds.

Feeding from ant hills is a relatively recent change in feeding habits. The woodpecker has developed a long tongue for extracting insects from bore holes deep in trees. However, it is equally useful in obtaining ants from the complicated tunnels of ant hills.

All woodpeckers are well adapted to obtaining their specialized food of various insects from the trunks and boughs of trees.

Adaptable Feet Feet are also adapted to feeding methods. In addition to the stiff and pointed tail feathers which support the woodpecker as it moves up a tree trunk, its feet have been adapted to give a powerful grip on the bark. Most small 'perching' birds have three toes in a forward position with the fourth toe at the rear. Woodpeckers, however, have two forward toes and two in the rear position.

The swift, spending most of its life on the wing,

landing on and taking off from vertical surfaces, has all four toes in the forward position.

The powerful talons of the barn owl are lethal to mice and voles, while the swimming feet of gulls, ducks, coots and grebes, although all different, are all perfectly adapted to every particular need.

The following adaptation, possessed by many birds, prevents them falling off a perch when asleep. When the legs are in the contracted position, that is, when 'sitting' on a branch rather than 'standing' on it, tendons in the legs pull the claws into a closed position and lock the bird on to the perch. When a bird is 'sitting' on a perch, try approaching it slowly. As the bird becomes more and more apprehensive of your approach, it will 'stand up' in order to depart from the perch quickly before it actually takes off. Usually its nervousness and the tension caused by approaching danger will cause it to defecate.

Left: Woodpeckers have developed very stiff and pointed tail feathers which support the bird as it moves up tree trunks. The feet of the woodpecker have also been adapted to give a powerful grasp on the bark of trees. Most small 'perching' birds have three toes in a for-ward position with the fourth toe to the rear. Woodpeckers, however, have two forward toes and two in the rear position.

Below: The hooked bill of the barn owl is used to rip up food. Its powerful talons are the weapons it uses to kill.

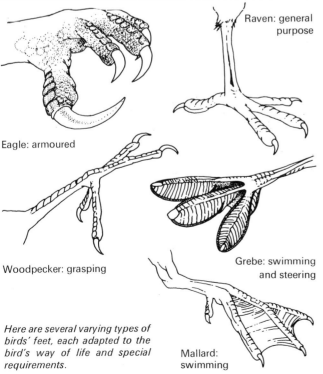

Raven: general purpose

Eagle: armoured

Woodpecker: grasping

Grebe: swimming and steering

Mallard: swimming

Here are several varying types of birds' feet, each adapted to the bird's way of life and special requirements.

Beaks and Bills Even casual observation of birds on a feeding table or in a park will show how even the commonest birds have adapted to the particular ways in which they acquire their food. It is hunting for, and consuming, food that directly or indirectly determine most of the adaptations in birds.

Beaks are obviously linked with the type of food the bird eats. The hooked beak of the bird of prey, the probing bill of the woodcock, the delicate pointed beak of the insect-eater and the general purpose bill of the omnivorous crow have developed as the bird's food becomes specialized.

The narrower the range of food taken by a bird, the more specialized its bill or beak tends to become. Where the method of feeding is similar, often the evolution of the bill has been paralleled in unrelated species. Similar bill shapes occur in kingfishers, terns, divers and grebes, gannets and herons – all use them for catching fish underwater. The fish-eating, diving ducks have refined an adaptation of the pointed bill. They have serrations along the edges of

Above: The swallow has a delicate beak with a wide gape to catch insects on the wing.

Below: The beak of the buzzard can tear the flesh of its prey. It is a formidable weapon.

the bill which earn them their name of 'Sawbills' – the mergansers, goosander and smew. There is a certain parallel between the shape of the curlew's bill and the curved beak of the tree creeper; whether the probing is among the mud, rocks and seaweeds of the seashore, or the cracks and crevices of a tree's bark, the function is similar. Of the many wading birds of the marsh and shore, there are numerous shapes and lengths of probing bill – but this variety means less competition. The long bills of godwits, curlews and snipe take worms and crustaceans from several inches down in the mud while shorter-billed birds feed at a lesser depth.

Above left: The carrion crow has an extremely powerful and accurate bill, which is suited to its use as a general purpose heavy chisel for the crow's omnivorous diet.

Above right: The woodcock has a collection of sensitive nerves at the tip of its bill enabling it to detect worms and crustaceans deep in semi-liquid mud. This bird was injured when it collided with telephone wires.

Centre left: The herring gull requires a bill for a similar type of scavenging diet to the crow: the bill is not dissimiliar in shape.

Centre right: The great crested grebe, seen here in its winter plumage, has a dagger-like bill with which it catches fish by diving beneath the surface.

Bottom left: This mistle thrush was possibly saved in a severe winter by apple peelings and cores. The mistle thrush has a beak suited to its 'soft food' diet of fruits, berries, worms and grubs.

Bottom right: This young spotted flycatcher, which has just made its first flight from the nest, shows the broad mouth and pointed beak of an insect-eater.

Winter Menu

There are certain severe conditions to which many birds are unable to adapt. You can help them survive by supplementing their meagre diet with the right kind of food in the bare winter months.

Bread and stale cake – soaked in water if very hard, except in frosty conditions.

Potato – leftovers or peelings boiled to a mash.

Meat – leftover scraps, poultry carcases, bones.

Fat – lumps, also useful for making a bird cake.

Apple – peelings and cores.

Sunflower heads – grown in a corner of the garden.

There are many ingenious ways of providing food for birds, and many relatively inexpensive products.

Peanuts (in shell) threaded on fine string.

Small plastic 'string' bags – hung up and filled with any scraps.

Large nails projecting from the feeding table on which pieces of bread can be speared.

One or two shelled nuts on fine thread will enable you to watch the dexterity of the small tits.

Fine mesh wire-netting can be used to make containers or can be tied over food on a branch.

'Birdcake', which consists of almost any leftovers – bacon rind, meat scraps, crumbled cake, chopped apple cores, nuts, stale sultanas or raisins and a handful of seed. Place ingredients in a basin, pour in melted fat and stir. Leave to cool and set.

Warning: never give birds salted nuts as they are unable to dispose of excess salt.

Feathers Birds are specialized animals in other ways, in addition to their adaptations to feeding. They are not unique in their ability to fly but the adaptation they possess which makes flight possible is a unique development. Only birds have feathers.

The major functions of feathers for most birds are the provision of wings and the conservation of a very high body temperature of about 41°C (106°F). Feathers are largely of two types: stiffly quilled or the softer, loosely webbed, body feathers. The lower half of these body feathers is downy and provides an insulating layer of warm air next to the bird's skin.

Flight feathers have a strong central shaft, on either side of which are two vanes, consisting of a close mesh of barbs and barbules hooked together. Primary flight feathers and most secondary feathers have a narrow vane (ie. the web of the feather) on the 'leading' edge of the feather, and a broader, more flexible vane on the 'trailing' edge. The narrow, firmer edge is lapped over the broad vane of the next feather so that on the down beat of the wing the vanes are pressed together providing resistance to the air. On the upward stroke the broad inner vane gives and twists, allowing air to pass through.

A feather examined under a lens or microscope will show what a complex and highly specialized structure it has become during bird evolution.

It is relatively easy to become familiar with the main types of feather and their position on a bird, once you start to look at feathers found on a woodland walk. You will find the most feathers in late summer, when birds are moulting. A close comparison of feathers found around the site of a 'kill', or examination of feathers found on a dead bird, will help you to develop an ability to recognize the origin of many feathers of common birds.

Because flight is necessary to escape from danger and for wide-ranging food-searching activities, together with the maintenance of temperature in adverse weather conditions, feather care is vital.

Preening – nibbling the feathers as they are passed through the beak – cleanses them of dirt and parasites. It is usually preceded by bathing, to dampen the feathers. Preening also helps to spread the preening oil, from the gland just above the tail, throughout the plumage to waterproof it. We call this gland the 'parson's nose' in poultry.

Observation of bathing birds will show that they follow a very definite toilet procedure. Dust bathing and sunning are also forms of toilet behaviour but there is little agreement about their function.

The intricate web of a feather is repaired by preening. Each split in a feather is 'zipped up' by rehooking the barbules of each barb to those of the next barb. It is easy to do this oneself to a split feather, by running the split between thumb and forefinger while, simultaneously, lifting the lower barb over and on to the one above.

Some birds have patches of continuously growing powder-down feathers close to the skin. The tips of these feathers disintegrate into a fine waterproof talc-like powder. This powder is particularly useful to fish-eating birds who are well supplied with powder-down feathers. The powder dries up the slime, with which the bird may have become covered, and thus assists in its removal.

Herons and bitterns have a serrated claw on the third toe which they use to comb the slime off the head and neck feathers.

Flight and wing shape The shape of a bird's wing is specifically adapted to meet the requirements of its own particular pattern of life. Watch

Above: This dead jay was a member of the crow family. It is specially adapted to flying in woods, with short, rounded wings and a largish, broad tail to help it steer, twisting and turning between the trees. Jays live in deciduous woods and feed on insects, seeds and buds.

Below: The Arctic tern breeds around the northern coasts of New England, Britain and Europe, up into the Arctic circle. Its grey underparts and long tail streamers are its most distinctive features. Here, in flight, with tail spread and wings 'braking', it tries to remain stationary.

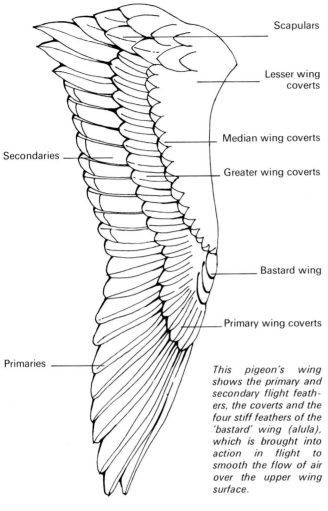

Scapulars

Lesser wing coverts

Median wing coverts

Greater wing coverts

Secondaries

Bastard wing

Primary wing coverts

Primaries

This pigeon's wing shows the primary and secondary flight feathers, the coverts and the four stiff feathers of the 'bastard' wing (alula), which is brought into action in flight to smooth the flow of air over the upper wing surface.

some gulls, with long, narrow, high-speed wings – masters of flight when there is space enough and steady wind but notice the difference in their performance when there is little wind and they are trying to land for food in the restricted space of a park or garden.

Watch pigeons – powerful fliers, with great endurance – take off with a noisy clatter as their wings clap together above and below their bodies.

The blackbird and the thrush are like the jay, magpie, sparrow hawk and pheasant in having short, rounded wings and a long tail. Although their rôles in the bird hierarchy are different, the one thing they have in common is the need to be able to fly fast through woodland, twisting through the branches of trees and bushes.

Some birds have 'specialized' in a general, all-purpose way and consequently have been very successful in adjusting to the changes that man has made to their natural environment. The starling feeds well on man's lawns, playing fields and pastures; these birds would not exist in the same way in a completely natural world.

The common or feral pigeon, descended from the wild rock dove whose natural home is among cliffs, has adopted the artificial cliffs of our cities, and now lives there only too successfully. Perhaps swifts would not be so numerous if there were not so many man-made cliffs from which they can take wing. This adaptation of bird life to a man-made environment is a good example of a bird's capacity to adjust.

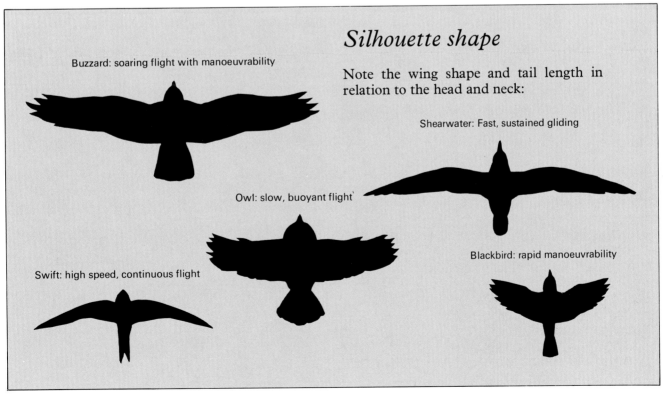

Silhouette shape

Note the wing shape and tail length in relation to the head and neck:

Buzzard: soaring flight with manoeuvrability

Shearwater: Fast, sustained gliding

Owl: slow, buoyant flight

Blackbird: rapid manoeuvrability

Swift: high speed, continuous flight

Nest Boxes

When setting up a nest box, there are some important general points to bear in mind:

Any wood 13 mm to 20 mm (0·5–0·8 in) thick will last longer than plywood.

Ensure that joints are as watertight as possible but drill drainage holes in the bottom.

Creosote or paint the box and weather it well before expected use. Fix in position in autumn or winter.

Site with entrance towards north-east (between north and south-east) away from sun and most rain.

Tilt with entrance down rather than up.

Hinge roof for inspection or cleaning. Rubber from an old rubber boot makes a good hinge. Roofing felt is a useful extra cover.

Fix securely to tree or support. If the tree is valuable, use a wooden dowling peg and do not drill too deeply.

Entrance sizes are crucial if you wish to exclude house sparrows (which require 32 mm [1·25 in]) from the smaller nest boxes with holes.

A

Open-fronted nest box: This is used by robin and wren or pied wagtail and spotted flycatcher. Which species use the box will depend upon siting – the first two birds require a concealed site below 1·20 m (4 ft). Pied wagtail and flycatcher prefer a more exposed situation. For flycatchers, the site should be higher – above 1·50 m (5 ft) up to 3·60 m (12 ft). Inside measurements: 11cm × 15cm (4½ in × 6 in).

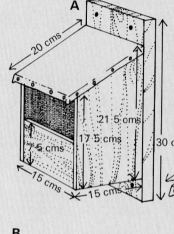

B

Nest box for tits and tree sparrow: Inside measurements: 11 cm × 15 cm (4½ in × 6 in). Entrance size: 25 mm (1 in) for blue tit, coal tit and marsh tit. 29 mm (1⅛ in) for great tit and tree sparrow. Holes that are larger than 29 mm (1⅛ in) will be dominated by house sparrows. Similarly, larger entrances (5 cm/2 in) will be used by starlings and woodpeckers.

C

Observation nest box – to be fixed inside a dark shed or hut. It is necessary to make a hole in the wall to correspond with the hole in the nest box. The sheet of glass should remain in place during observation. With the shed door shut (and window blackened out) quietly remove the hardboard and watch. Size according to species.

D

Nest box for swallow: Site under eaves, in open outhouse and barns. May also be used by unorthodox blackbirds.

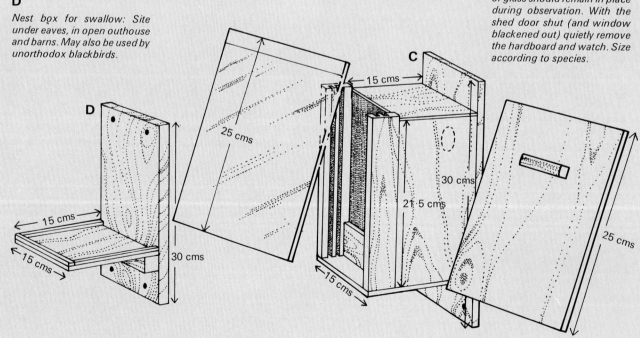

Nest boxes Although many birds, such as the pigeon and swift, have freely adapted to new conditions, others can benefit from a certain amount of help from man. Nest boxes are a means of attracting useful birds into your garden and thus reducing the number of insect pests. You will also help in the conservation of some species of birds where a shortage of suitable nest sites may drive them from the area.

Colouring Nesting boxes and feeding tables are interesting ways of bringing birds to you so that you may watch them at odd moments and in comfort. Differences in colouring may be one of the first things to strike you. A combination of natural and sexual selection accounts for the different colourings and ornaments which distinguish the sexes.

The most attractive males are also the most successful in threatening other males and thus defending a nesting territory. The females who have the most successful camouflage are the ones most likely to escape predators and rear a family. In species where the sexes are both brightly coloured, as in the European robin, both birds defend a territory and need a red breast with which to threaten intruding robins.

Where both sexes have similar colours and markings it will usually be found that both play roles with some degree of equal responsibility in attending the nest, eggs and young. When the males are strikingly different from the females and brightly coloured, they are usually very territorial or elaborate in the sexual displays which accompany pairing ceremonies. Displays take place in some species where there is no sex-plumage difference – such as the grebes or cranes – but in these cases the females take part in the display. In some species with similar plumage but a different territorial role, the difference is vocal rather than of feathers – the male sings.

Right: Introduced into many countries as a game bird, and now breeding in a feral situation in Britain, Europe and North America, is the Asiatic pheasant. In the photograph the cock is displaying his bright colours, including the red skin on his face, to 'threaten' the camera. The incubating female has camouflage colouring for protection against predators. Cocks display a wide variation in colouring.

Above left: A pair of mallard ducks. The brightly coloured drake does not help the female incubate the eggs. His striking plumage is used in pairing and territorial displays, whereas the well-camouflaged female escapes attention when sitting on the eggs. During June and July the drake's plumage changes and he resembles the duller female. This is called the 'eclipse' plumage and is adopted by several species of duck. Drakes are in 'eclipse' at the time of moult, when for a few weeks the loss of flight feathers makes escape by flying impossible. During this period camouflage is essential for the drake and has obvious survival value.

Above right: The tufted duck, like a similar and closely related ring-necked duck of North America, is a diving duck. The drakes are strikingly coloured whereas the drably plumaged female can safely sit on her eggs unseen in the shadows of a reed bed. Tufted ducks are widespread in Britain and northern Europe as they are both resident breeders and migrants.

What to see when you look Colouring is only one method of distinguishing birds and not always the most satisfactory. You may be content to enjoy watching without surrounding yourself with identification books – one day, however, you will see a strange bird you have not seen before and want to know what it is. Describing what you actually saw is not easy without some basic knowledge. The drawings on this page will help you to remember which part of the bird was white or streaked. You may also need to know *what to notice*.

Size is a most useful point. Birds remain the same size throughout their adult lives, not changing except when they fluff up their feathers. Accurate observation is assisted by comparison with a bird which you know. Was it larger or smaller than a robin, or a blackbird or a pigeon?

The general shape of the bird should be noted – whether the tail was short or long, whether the wings were pointed or rounded. Movement and behaviour are also sometimes significant. Did it walk or hop? Did it often flick its wings or tail?

Small but distinctive markings are sometimes essential to notice. Did it have a pale eye stripe? Did it have a white rump or white outer tail feathers? Wing pattern can also be important to record.

Sometimes colour can be an obstacle to identification as it changes with the light. Two people do not always see colour in the same way, and the bird's colour varies with the season. Do not be too dogmatic about the colour you see.

Often the time of year will eliminate many possibilities. A bird described as a summer visitor is unlikely to be seen before the beginning of April or after mid-October in the northern hemisphere; a winter visitor is equally unlikely after April or before October.

It will frequently happen that you cannot identify the bird because the light was not good, the bird was too quick, or you failed to notice a vital detail. Do not be too concerned – your skill will increase, although there will often be times when you miss something. This will happen less frequently as you become more experienced.

A quick and simple way to record details of a bird you have seen is to sketch it. The following method of drawing a bird in a variety of positions may make it easier for you to note its main characteristics. Do not worry if your artistic skill is limited – all that matters is that you record the basic positions of the markings on a bird. In any case, your skill will grow with practice.

Above: The binocular vision of these little owls is an advantage in hunting. An ability to judge distance quickly and accurately is vital to a hunter. This owl is more likely to be seen in daylight than most: it frequents country-side which is well scattered with trees. Its strange, mournful yelp-ing cry is so characteristic that it is the best indication of its pres-ence. Like all owls, it has both broad wings and a wide wing span. Because of its colouring a good pair of binoculars are needed to spot it.

Binoculars

Binoculars are necessary when your interest in bird-watching develops and you wish to see and know more.

Binoculars are the only essential piece of equipment but they are expensive and therefore it is important to make the right choice.

Binoculars are described as 8 × 30 or 10 × 50 and so on. The first of these two figures tells you the magnification – eight times or ten times – but the larger the magnification, the smaller will be the area you can see, making it difficult to find birds in foliage. The second number is the diameter of the object lens in millimetres; this is the lens you point at the bird. The size of this lens is important in determining the light-gathering power of the binoculars. Thus, a pair of binoculars 8 × 30 will not enable you to see as large an area or so well in a poor light as a pair of 8 × 40.

The relationship between the two numbers is the vital factor to know. Divide the first figure into the second – any result between 4 and 7 is acceptable. On the seashore or moorland, a higher magnification is needed – at least 10 × – thus, 10 × 40 or 10 × 50 which give a light gathering value of 4 and 5 is suitable. In woodland and countryside 8 × is sufficient – 8 × 30 or 8 × 40, also giving light-gathering values of approximately 4 and 5, are what you require.

Beware of buying the cheapest binoculars without looking at others. When you have decided on the power you need, compare the most expensive pair with the cheapest; test them in an area of bad light, looking for clarity and definition at the edge.

Trees through the Seasons

In the temperate parts of the world, a seasonal pattern of winter, spring, summer and autumn occurs, and that pattern is closely associated in our minds with trees.

There are frequent instances in folklore where trees such as the oak, ash, holly and yew are said to have magical powers and connections with ancient gods. In Greece the oak was thought to be sacred to Zeus, in Rome to Jupiter, in Norway to Thor an in Germany to Thunor. Hawthorn (May) blossom was widely used in the May-time fertility cult and was associated with a 'green' man decorated with foliage. This custom has its origins in the beliefs of the first cultivators of the soil. While in North America, the Indians worshipped the giant sequoias as gods.

The patterns and forms of trees in the landscape dominate the memory of walking in the woods and countryside in winter. The first signs that indicate the beginning of spring are the swelling buds and catkins of trees, and the height of spring is symbolized by tree blossom. Thoughts of summer invariably include the cool shade of trees, while autumn, to most people, means little more than the time of year when trees lose their leaves – the fall.

Two or three centuries ago, in order to find more than a dozen species of tree in a day's walking through the countryside, it would have been necessary to pass through changes in landscape and soil. The number of trees that are natural and native to an area is usually very small. Many of the trees in gardens, parks, estates and even planted forests are trees that have been introduced from elsewhere by man – sometimes from as far away as the other side of the world.

Although there are related trees in both the Old World and the New World, there is only one species which is found in both, and that is the common juniper. Birches, poplars, oaks, maples, elms and many of the conifers are represented as families in both zones. Most of the species occurring in Britain are also found all over Europe and often well into Asia, but probably only the English elm is endemic – or native – only to Britain and nowhere else in the world.

There are many European trees which did not occur naturally in Britain until introduced by man. The sweet chestnut and walnut were perhaps two of

Upper far left: The 'conker' tree, or horse chestnut, grows as a native in northern Greece and was introduced to Britain early in the seventeenth century. The well-known and beautiful flower spikes of the horse chestnut are as much a sign of spring as its popular nuts are a sign of autumn. Each flower has long stamens curving downwards and the stigma is on a short stem, so pollination is by visiting bees from another flower. The red horse chestnut is a hybrid variety and is propagated by grafting.

Upper near left: The sweet chestnut is in no way related to the horse chestnut. The tree is native to southern Europe, north Africa and western Asia. Most nuts eaten in Britain are imported.

Lower far left: This strawberry tree is a rare tree which is native to western Ireland, and has been introduced elsewhere into parks. The fruit is edible but unpleasant. It is also a native of the western Mediterranean area, having reached Ireland before

the British Isles were separated from western Europe. It has survived in Ireland because of the warm, moist climate.

Lower near left: Walnut trees grow across south-eastern Europe in to Asia and China. The Romans introduced the walnut to Europe. It resembles an ash superficially – in bark, twig, bud and leaf – but the leaves grow alternately.

Opposite top: These ancient pollarded beeches are growing in old woodland that in mediaeval times was a hunting forest for Kings. The practice of pollarding ensured that new growth was beyond the reach of browsing deer. The trunks are therefore old, but the branches are little more than a hundred years old.

Opposite bottom: This picture of old beech woodland shows trees, pollarded a century ago, which were once the coppice growth from an older tree's stump that has long gone.

the first, introduced by the Romans. The last Ice Age retreated north across Europe comparatively recently, allowing only five or six thousand years for trees to spread back to Britain before the land was separated from Europe; the beech may have been the last tree to reach Britain naturally.

Anywhere – in town, park, garden, countryside or forest – trees are living records of the past. Sometimes the shelter belt of sycamores planted around a daleside farmhouse will date the house. The age of trees in a planted woodland, or the stumps of earlier trees, the ages of trees in a park or a churchyard, or the size and age of trees in a hedge will all help to establish a broader and deeper picture of one's surroundings. Sometimes, also, the known age of a building may help in assessing the age of a tree. Often, the relative growth rates of different species of trees, if planted when a new town was established, can be calculated.

Most trees in the countryside are there because man put them there or allowed them to stay if they grew there unaided. Usually, they have been 'managed' – this will apply to woodland or hedgerow. Often, they have influenced their surroundings or they have been affected by what has happened around them: sometimes as a result of man's activities, sometimes due to their natural environment – to erosion or exposure, or a stream or other trees. As your powers of observation increase and questioning what you see becomes second nature, the accuracy of your interpretative skills will also grow.

One of the oldest forms of woodland management is coppicing; that is, cutting a tree down to ground level. This produces a growth of shoots around the stump which are harvested at regular intervals, according to the species and its rate of growth and the size of pole required. Coppice-with-standards, a form of woodland management that goes back to mediaeval times, involved coppicing most trees of a species – for example, sweet chestnut, hazel or alder – and allowing 'standards' of perhaps oak or ash or elm to grow to full mature height in order to provide the larger structural timbers required in those days for building houses.

The practice of pollarding ('beheading') a tree is just as old. Oak, ash and willow were commonly pollarded in hedgerows. The new shoots then grew between two and three metres above the ground and beyond the reach of browsing cattle or deer. A crop would also be taken from this growth at regular intervals. In some ancient woodlands this was the traditional practice. Both pollarding and coppicing are thought to prolong the life of the tree – certainly some pollards and coppice stumps are hundreds of years old.

One of the striking things about a deciduous tree in winter is the silhouette it makes against the sky. There are three aspects of this. Firstly, there is the general shape of the tree, which may be quite characteristic; for instance, the silver birch, which, when mature, droops at the ends of the branches, is a familiar shape, but other trees are equally distinctive. The elm has a tall, straight bole that billows out with a great domed head of foliage which gives the branches distinct contours. The Italian black poplar has an open widespread fingers shape.

Secondly, there is the character that the growth of the branches gives to the shape of the tree. The branches of an English oak twist and turn erratically; more graphically described in the words of a child, they are 'all elbows and knees'. Different again is the horse chestnut, where the branches sag from the tree gracefully before they sweep up again at the ends.

Finally, there is the pattern made by the twigs – the stabbing skywards sprays that square off the top of a beech, or the delicate criss-cross tracery of the lime, or the coarser, squared pattern of oak twigs continuing the character of the branches.

Having looked from a distance, it is then necessary to go closer to look at the form of a twig. Are the buds alternate on the twig or are they opposite each other? Some of the buds are more than just leaf buds – they are shoots that, by the end of the following summer, will have become twigs themselves with buds. Look again, are the buds that are opposite each other (in pairs) going to grow in the same direction as the next pair or is there a 90 degree change? Are the buds that are alternate all growing in the same plane or are they arranged spirally, if you look at the twig end-on?

The character of the twig growth must be repeated in the small branches and has, in the past, contributed to the way the larger branches and boughs have developed.

But there is still more to see on a twig. Look below the buds, there should be the scar where a leaf was attached last summer. It is best to start looking at trees with larger twigs, such as the ash and horse chestnut. Look for the little gathering of 'girdle rings' around the twig. Starting from the tip, it should be possible to trace back the growth of a spray of twigs. It may be that the distance between each set of rings will vary. This distance represents the growth during one season; a short distance should coincide with a dry summer and, conversely, a wet summer with good growth will mean a greater distance between the rings.

An exceptionally dry summer may well have also been a hotter summer. Sometimes this encourages the tree to produce more fruiting buds and, providing the *following* spring is without frosts at the time of fertilization and that the next summer is wet enough for fruit to grow, a bumper fruit or seed crop

*Far left: Five trees can be identified in the photograph by their shape and branching. Three elms (*Ulmus carpinifolia) *are growing in the foreground with Scots pines on the right and in the distance. Lombardy poplars are easily identifiable in the centre and middle distance. An oak stands behind (left) the Lombardy poplars and, in the far distance, the rather spiky growth of young Italian black poplars can be seen.*

Near left: This beech, on an exposed road, shows the effect of persistent wind. It is 'fixed' in that position.

Upper near right: Ash branches have few twigs and the side and lower branches curve upwards.

Upper far right: The hornbeam has a fine tracery of twigs but it is easy to identify by the snaky silver lines on the bark of the main boughs and branches.

Lower near right: The silver birch is distinguished from the downy, or hairy, birch at a distance by the drooping ends of its branches. The 'warty' name for the silver birch refers to little white warts on the twigs while the downy, or hairy, birch has twigs which are covered with fine white hairs.

Lower far right: Beech twigs, with their characteristic pointed orange buds, are also quite distinct and easy to recognize at a distance, as the long 'sprays' of twigs and buds curve upwards.

should result in the autumn. Thus, the sayings which suggest that a hard winter will follow from a great number of berries and seeds on the trees is putting the cart before the horse! All that might be deduced is that the *previous* summer (the year before) was one that stimulated the trees into producing flowers or fruiting buds; it may also follow that less growth occurred at the end of the twig during that summer.

Sometimes, accurate assumptions can be made about past summers by an examination of the annual growth rings of a stump or a cut log. Besides the well-known fact that the number of rings indicates the age of the tree, the width of a ring, wide or narrow, reflects the weather of that particular summer. Every year, a tree grows another layer on the outer side of its trunk, boughs, branches and twigs; growth rings will show in twigs that are more than one year old. The bark of a tree consists of three layers: the old dead bark layers on the outside, 'cork'; the living layer of the bark, 'green bark'; the third and inner layer, 'the bast'. Between the bark and the wood of the tree is a thin, wet, usually green

layer of living cells called cambium. Bark can be stripped from a living twig if a length is cut off – elderberry strips very easily – so that this may be seen. Inside the cambium or 'growth' layer is the wood; the outer rings are the 'sap wood' and the inner core of rings, usually darker and stronger, is the 'heart wood'.

Every year the cells of the cambium layer grow new layers of cells on the sapwood and on the inside of the bast layer. So each year the circumference of the sap wood increases and the bark layer increases from the inside. In the spring, when the buds and leaves are opening and growing, greater quantities of sap are required. At this time the cambium layer grows conductive tissues – 'spring wood'. Later, when growth slows down, more solid cells are formed with less conductive tissue – 'summer wood'. It is the differences between these two types of tissue which make the lighter part of the annual ring (the spring wood), gradually darken (summer) and then change suddenly when all growth stops during the winter months. If you can, look at a tree-stump and examine the different rings and layers.

Left: Horse chestnut twig and bud, because of their large size, show clearly such features as the bud scales, the horseshoe-shaped leaf scars (dotted where veins were), and the girdle rings, which indicate where one year's growth finishes and another starts.

Right: The horse chestnut buds are well known as 'sticky buds'; because they are large, the unfolding of the hairy leaves is fascinating to observe day by day as it becomes more rapid.

An inspection of twigs in the winter will show buds and catkins already formed and waiting for the following spring – for instance, birch and hazel catkins for next year can be found before the leaves fall this year. In early spring, when the soil temperature rises sufficiently (above 40°F/5°C) and the days are long enough, fine hair roots will start growing again and the sap will be drawn up through the tubes and pores of the sapwood and the cambium layer. Water and minerals will be supplied to the buds, which will swell; the dark scales on the buds start to separate, the buds break and the leaves unfurl and the complex process of manufacturing food begins.

The green pigment, chlorophyll, in the leaves begins to make carbohydrates – the starch and sugars using the sunlight, water and carbon dioxide from the air. During this process the leaves release oxygen into the air. As the water and nutrients are drawn up the trunk from the roots, so some of the manufactured carbohydrates go down through the bast layer to feed and be stored in the roots. The entire process is called 'photosynthesis'. When daylight diminishes, it stops and the complicated exchange of gases reverses the balance – oxygen is used up and carbon dioxide released into the air.

Something else begins to happen in the spring when the leaves unfold – some buds may be larger and fatter than others and they contain more than leaves.

Almost all trees are flowering trees. The conifers are in a sense different in that the seeds are not enclosed in an ovary, but they have pollen-bearing organs and separate seed-bearing growths which become the cones. It is often convenient to refer to them as 'flowers'.

It is also convenient to describe the pollen organs or the ovule and seed-bearing parts of all flowers as 'male' and 'female' respectively.

Most of the trees that are thought of as having blossom – the fruit trees, blackthorn, hawthorn and rowan, etc. – have flowers which contain the pollen bearing anthers on the end of stamens. They also

Above: Minute flowers of the blackthorn or sloe are usually the first flowers of the hedgerow or thicket that are noticed. The black twigs of the bushes are usually covered by the massed white blossom before the leaves appear. In this close-up photograph, the flowers show the pollen-bearing, orange-topped stamens, while in the centre is a long greenish style, the tip of which, the stigma, collects pollen. Fertilized by insects, the base of the flower develops into the sloe – a small plum-like fruit with a rough, astringent taste.

Below and below right: Hazel flowers appear very early on the twigs. These familiar catkins are a long series of little clusters of male pollen-bearing flowers. The female flowers must be searched for – they appear to be small green buds with a little tuft of crimson spikes. These are the stigmas and, if fertilized, this is where the hazel nuts will grow. Male catkins, which will flower in the spring of the following year, are already well formed when the bunches of nuts are ripening on the branches in September.

contain a pistil, consisting of a style which has a stigma on the end to collect pollen. The pistil contains an ovary which becomes a seed 'box'. These male and female parts are contained in the centre of one single flower (hermaphrodite) and each, if fertilized, is capable of producing seed.

There are trees which, like the conifers, bear separate male and female flowers on the same tree (monœcious). The seeds are, of course, grown only in the female flowers. The birch, oak, beech, hornbeam, hazel, alder and walnut are all included in this group. There are other trees such as the willows and poplars, the yew and holly which have separate male flowers on one tree and female flowers on another (diœcious): so, in these species, a tree bearing seed is a 'female' tree, while the other, 'male', trees can never develop seed.

An examination of the flowers of these trees with a lens will show which 'sex' they are. Generally speaking, flowers which are bi-sexual – termed 'perfect' flowers – are pollinated by insects. Those with uni-sexual flowers, either on the same tree or on separate trees, are usually wind pollinated. The conifers are included – having both flowers on one tree. An exception to this are some willows, such as the goat willow or sallows, which are also visited by insects. There are some confusing cases, however. For example in some of the maples and the ash, the flowers are capable of being either bi-sexual or uni-sexual. Frequently, one cluster of flowers on a tree will contain each sex in separate flowers in the same cluster; or sometimes a branch will have flowers belonging wholly to one sex or the other.

There are various ways of avoiding self pollination. Sometimes the time of pollen release and ripening of the stigma are not synchronized. Sometimes the female flowers grow higher or lower on the tree and, in certain cases, on the very ends of the branches. In all trees where flowers are one or other sex, the male flowers wither and drop off after the release of pollen. It is the male pollen-bearing catkins that litter the ground under poplars, willows, oaks and beeches.

Above: The opening of delicate, green beech leaves in spring is quickly accompanied by the appearance of the male catkins – little balls of stamens hanging on a slender, hairy stem. The upright female flower has greenish stigmas surrounded by a cluster of red 'hairs'. These female flowers usually appear after their neighbouring male catkins have finished distributing their pollen. In this way there is a greater chance of cross-pollination between trees by wind-blown pollen. Like the catkins of many trees in spring, the male catkins litter the ground under the trees after releasing pollen.

Below left and below: The willows have their male and female flowers growing on different trees. The male (left) and the female (right) catkins of the goat willow, or sallow, are commonly called 'pussy willow', because of the silvery hairs of the male flowers before they are fully open. Willows are largely fertilized by insects. This willow is sometimes known as the 'palm' willow because it is used in churches on Palm Sunday.

The form of growth of the lower branches of a tree is different from that of the upper branches and, in one sense, they are specialized. Sitting on the ground beneath the lower branches of a spreading beech on a sunny day will make obvious the economical spread of the leaves, where each has taken a small patch of light so effectively that little light gets through the mosaic of leaves. Those leaves on the upper branches receive light from several directions and so do not hold themselves so rigidly or in the same plane as the lowest branches do.

An examination of the stalks of leaves will reveal differences that challenge investigation. Aspen and poplar leaves are well known for their rustling and quivering in the lightest of breezes; a close look at the leaf stalks and it will be obvious why aspens move when others are still. Many species with large leaves have stalks and leaf-veins, which, in section, are semi-circular or 'U' shaped, providing extra strength. The stems of other large leaves have developed a very broad base, which gives strong attachment to the twig and considerable protection to the adjoining bud.

There are other differences between the top of a tree and the lower branches besides those caused by the availability of light. For example, the temperature can be very different. Again, the wind strength will be greater at the top and so the upper leaves must offer less resistance. Often there is a considerable difference in time between the opening of the upper and lower buds because of this. It is not necessarily always the same – sometimes the wind or sun can have an opposite effect.

The change of colour and fall of leaves will also vary between the top and bottom of the tree for the same varying reasons.

Above left: The European larch, like all larches, is deciduous – it drops its needles before the winter, and grows them afresh in the spring. A decorative and valuable timber tree, it has been introduced to many countries (to Britain in the early seventeenth century), but is native to the Alps and the Carpathians and other central European mountainous areas. The photograph shows the immature cones; at an earlier age, they are a delicate cerise pink.

Above right: The field maple fruits, like the fruits of all the many species of maple, are winged and can be carried considerable distances by strong winds. The fruits are in pairs but they fall singly, spinning as they do so. The field maple is native to Britain, most of Europe and southwest Asia.

Below left: The sallow or goat willow develops its seed early. Before summer has begun, the pod-like fruit on the catkins have burst, dispersing the hairy seeds, which look like cotton down. The name 'goat willow' derives from the fact that it is readily browsed by grazing animals, especially goats. The goat willow can be found in many parts of Britain and Europe and also in western Asia.

Below right: The spindle has most distinctive and attractive fruit. These are pink and four-lobed and, when the capsule splits open, bright orange seeds are revealed. The name originates from the use of the wood for spindles. The plant occurs on lime rich soil all over Britain, Europe and western Asia and also, to some extent, in North America. The bark, leaves and fruit are poisonous.

Leaves contain a yellow pigment as well as the green of chlorophyll. Leaves that die in summer lose the green pigment but remain yellow. It is not fully understood what triggers the autumn change. The chlorophyll and other minerals are returned into the tree and a layer of cork cells is formed between the leaf and the twig. The variation in colour between species of trees and between similar trees, or between different leaves on the same tree, is caused by differing amounts of various chemicals left in the leaf and the effect of the weather, the sun and the air upon them. The growth of the cork seals the joint and secures the tree against water loss and fungal infection. Eventually, the wind, rain, or the weight of frost crystals causes the leaf to fall.

Evergreen trees, although shedding odd leaves all the year round, shed most leaves in the spring – but leaves are retained for more than a year. They are able to resist frost because of their greater oil and wax content, and the slippery surface of many evergreen leaves enables the tree to avoid damage by shedding snow more easily. Conifers solve the problem with their narrow needles which are advantageous in several ways: the needles offer less resistance to the wind or snow and they conserve water better. For these reasons the trees are able to grow in exposed situations.

Like leaves, seeds, too, must come off trees. This is usually achieved by two agencies – wind and animals (including birds). There are many very effective winged seeds, – those of the maples, sycamore, ash, birch, hornbeam, elm and lime. Poplars and willows also use the wind by developing 'plumed' or 'feathered' seeds. The trees that produce fruit or nuts are dependent on the birds or animals who eat the fruit and consequently the seed which passes through them. Other fruits, such as those of the beech, oak, sweet and horse chestnuts and hazel, are certainly eaten by animals but it is only indirectly that some survive uneaten, having been carried from the parent tree. For example, squirrels and jays take acorns and bury them and, more often than not, the acorns are 'forgotten'. Other nuts are buried, too, or merely dropped for one reason or another. Conifer seeds are winged and so are primarily distributed by the wind but some must also be dropped by animals and birds – either the seeds or the cones.

Assessing the age of a tree without counting the growth rings – that is, without cutting it down – is difficult but possible. Alan Mitchell (see Booklist) gives a simple rule: he states that the mean growth in circumference or girth (measured 1·5 m [5 ft] above the ground) of trees that still have a full crown is 2·5 cm (1 in) per year. This remains true of most species: early growth is faster than later growth.

Above: Hazel nuts, in their green cups, ripen in August and September and then fall from the cups to the ground. A popular food of small animals and birds, many nuts are carried away to be eaten or stored; enough are dropped or lost to propagate the tree. It is native to most of Europe, Asia Minor and North Africa

Below: The plum-like fruit of the blackthorn is the sloe. The fruit has a very bitter, rough taste that is less unpleasant after frost; it is used in making wine and flavouring gin. If the sloes are picked in autumn, pricked and infused with sugar in gin and shaken occasionally, the liqueur will be ready for Christmas.

Plants without Flowers

Trees may be the largest plants on earth but the smallest are more ancient. There are six groups of plants that most people do not even think of when the word 'plant' is mentioned; yet for four hundred million years – until a hundred million years ago – they were the only land plants growing on this planet.

The first plants with flowers began to develop, significantly, with the evolution and appearance of insects as we know them. It was only 50 million years ago that the evolution of flowering plants exploded with variations and adaptations that enabled them to become the dominant form of vegetation that they are today.

Until that time, the earth's plant life was largely made up of what are loosely called 'flowerless plants'. This group includes the algae, fungi, lichens, liverworts, mosses, ferns and their related species.

If viruses can be said to cover the hazy area of definition between living and non-living things, then bacteria fill the gap of definition between plants and animals, at a microscopic level. Bacteria are usually classified as plants and may be observed with a microscope.

Reproduction in ferns, fungi, liverworts, lichens, mosses and algae is by spores instead of by seeds. Spores are single cells that are microscopic in size and are produced in vast numbers. In the case of liverworts, mosses and ferns, those in suitable conditions grow into plants by cell division (gametophytes). These plants eventually produce male and female organs, either on the same plant or, in some cases, on separate plants. Male cells find their way to the female egg cells. The fertilized egg or zygote then becomes an embryonic plant (sporophyte) which grows and develops a fruiting capsule producing spores, thus completing the cycle of alternate generations.

The single cell spores are released in great quantities on the basis that the greater the number released, the greater will be the chance of a few spores finding the right conditions. Although this may seem to be haphazard, the spores are often released only when exactly the right conditions are affecting the fruiting body.

We often think of algae as tiny green plants, many of which grow in water. Most algae require the observer to use a microscope before they can be seen individually. However, there are very large plants that are also algae. These are the common seaweeds.

The smallest algae are the single-celled forms that float freely and, in early summer, turn water green. There are many kinds, some of which form green slime on the surfaces of rocks, sand and plants under the water and others that form threads or filaments which, when very numerous, are referred to as 'blanket weed'. All these algae are intricate and

fascinating to examine under a microscope.

There are also algae that live out of water. The most familiar is the bright green, powdery, single-celled algae called Pleurococcus which covers the moister side of tree trunks.

All algae possess chlorophyll and, by the process of photosynthesis, make food from carbon dioxide, water and sunlight.

As they have no chlorophyll, fungi are plants that have no roots, leaves or flowers. Lichens are a combination of two plants – a fungus and an alga. The tangle of fungus threads forms a sponge-like body with groups of single-celled algae distributed throughout them. By living together they comple-

ment each other; the fungus can absorb and hold water, while the alga can create food. In this way, the combination plant, the lichen, can exist in situations where neither the fungus nor the alga could live separately; for instance, on bare dry rock where there is little or no moisture until rain falls, and where there is no food except that manufactured from sunlight by photosynthesis.

Lichens can be found in extreme conditions – on the sea shore on rocks above the tide-line but in the splash zone, in the Arctic and the Antarctic regions, on acid moorland, on mountain rocks, on logs, trees and branches in sunlit woodlands, and even on dry walls and roofs in towns that are not polluted with smoke. Some species of lichen are more tolerant of smoke-polluted air than others and, by grading certain species by their tolerance, it has proved possible to use their presence or absence as indicators of pollution levels in selected areas. Lichens have been found growing at 6,000 metres (20,000 feet) on Mount Everest. They take several forms, which can be categorized as follows: there are the crusty forms which grow on tree trunks, walls, roofs and rocks; the more leafy types that grow in similar places; the erect and upright forms often shaped like a cup; and the hairy and feathery species that grow mostly on trees. They are extremely slow growing, and some patches are thought to be almost as old as the oldest trees.

Above: Most people think of algae as green slime that grows in aquaria and ponds in spring and early summer. This occurs especially if the water is 'new' or too rich in minerals from fertilizers which have drained from the land during the winter.

Left: In a moist, warm, wooded valley ferns, mosses, liverworts and lichens almost completely cover the rocks. Bilberries or blueberries also act as a ground cover to the wood. The mosses are bright green and the lichens are grey-green and almost black.

Near top right: The lichens that grow on trees in clean air areas, free from sulphur dioxide smoke pollution, assume quite a different form. The most attractive are the feathery branching species (Usnea spp.). Frequently, branches and twigs of trees are festooned with these lichens. Many groups of lichens are attractive and develop unusual forms when mature. For example, Cladoniae are usually erect in one form or another. They often grow cup-like structures which are dusted with reproductive granules (a vegetative or sexual form) which can develop into new plants. Bright red or brown fruiting structures grow on the cups and release capsules which contain many spores (sexual reproduction).

Far top right: Algae do not grow only in water; a dry powdery form called Pleurococcus grows on trees and forms the bright green areas shown in the photograph. The grey-green patches that accompany it are lichen of a species that is more tolerant than most of air pollution by smoke and can even be found in cities.

Near bottom right: Lichens on trees are more familiar in this leafy form on a hedgerow-oak. The old saying that moss always grows on the 'north side' of a tree is not necessarily true – both mosses and lichens grow best on the moistest side, i.e. the side most sheltered from wind and sun.

Far bottom right: On this rock, which is just above the high tide line on the seashore, are at least four lichens that are peculiar to the particular conditions of what is known as the 'splash-zone'.

*Top left: The fleshy fronds (thallus) in this specimen of liverwort (*Marchantia*) are dotted with little cups or goblets which contain the 'gemmae', small embryonic plants which are a form of vegetative reproduction.*

Top right: The liverwort Marchantia polymorpha. *Liverworts are simple plants, for apart from the reproductive cells there is little specialization by other cells – most have no roots, stem or leaves, nerve or midrib and thus no conductive tissue of any kind. The microscopic male cells are bounced off the flat-topped male organs by raindrops and are caught in the ribs of the female organs. These are shown in the photograph.*

Above left: The crescent-cup liverwort is another common species. Here it shows the reason for its name: the cups contain the 'gemmae'. This liverwort grows on the banks of streams.

Above right: The other form in which liverworts grow is rather more like a moss. The fruiting bodies are shown in the photograph – those that have burst and have shed their spores show as four-sided brown stars.

Below: The juniper-leaved hair moss is common on heaths, especially after burning or where there is bare ground. The four-sided spore capsules are hooded by large hairy calyptras until the spores are nearly ripe.

Liverworts are very green plants and usually only grow in damp or wet places. They are divided into two groups, one of which (the leafy liverworts) looks rather like a moss. They can often be found along the wetter parts of the banks of a stream or river, on damp paths, moist bare soil, old logs, where water runs over rocks and even in humid greenhouses.

The easier group of liverworts to recognize consists of flatly gathered clusters of fleshy green 'leaves' which are attached to a moist surface by minute, root-like threads. The most common species of this type are *Pellia epiphylla*, the crescent cup liverwort (*Lunularia cruciata*) and *Marchantia polymorpha*. The leafy liverworts are best looked at with a small lens as they may appear to be mosses to the untrained eye. They grow in long fronds with a row of flat leaf-like parts on either side which, as with all liverworts, do not have mid-ribs nor roots, stems, nerves or leaves.

Liverworts with mosses make up a group of plants called the *Bryophytae*, whose reproductive processes require water. Reproduction, as has been stated, is by alternating generations – sexual reproduction. However, apart from pieces breaking off and forming new plants, there is another method of vegetative or asexual reproduction which occurs in liverworts. 'Buds', or gemmae, are formed on the main leafy part of the thallus of the plant. Sometimes these are formed in little cups, and sometimes they grow in little clusters on the ends of the 'leaves'. The 'buds', or gemmae, are carried away from the parent plant by rain or by splashing water and, if deposited in the right place – the ribs of the female organs – may form new plants.

Mosses are less dependent on water than are liverworts and are more uniform in structure. Most mosses have very thin leaves, often only one cell thick, with no special outer layer or cuticle and so they are very sensitive to the degree of humidity. The leaves frequently have a mid-rib or nerve and are usually arranged spirally around the stem. Unlike liverworts, mosses often grow as separate male and female plants. In many mosses, one stem with its crowning rosette of leaves constitutes one whole plant – thus, a tuft of moss is made up of many plants.

It is in the rosette at the top of the stem that the sexual organs develop, sometimes both on the same stem but more often on separate stems. Reproduction is similar to that of liverworts; the male cells also require a film of water on the plant to enable them to swim to the female organ. Some mosses also resemble liverworts in their method of vegetative reproduction.

Most ferns take the form of the popular concept

of a fern; that is, of large feathery fronds which unroll from the tip as they grow. The fronds are usually divided into leaflets (pinnate) which are often divided again (bipinnate) and in several species divided yet again (tripinnate). The reproductive cycle of alternating generations is similar to mosses and liverworts. The spores are produced in pin-head sized capsules or spore cases (sporangia) which grow in tight button-shaped groups (sori) on the underside of certain leaflets.

The common bracken, which can grow in drier and sunnier situations than most ferns is so successful and deep-rooted that it is a major problem to farmers when clearing land. The sori form a continuous line along the edge of the underside of leaflets. July and August are the best time of year to inspect the underside of fern fronds for the sori. The tiny spores are distributed in millions; those that land in a moist situation develop into a flat plate of green tissue (prothallus) less than 2 cm (1 inch) across, rather like a small liverwort. This prothallus merely grows separate male and female organs. From the fertilized egg the new fern plant develops and the prothallus gradually withers away.

Some ferns have long, undivided leaves such as the Hartstongue fern, while in Australia and New Zealand great tree ferns can grow to a height of 20 metres (65 feet). The tiny North American water fern, azolla, introduced into this country at the turn of the century, and which looks like a fleshy, leafy liverwort, about duckweed size, can spread in a mass over the surface of a pond or lake very quickly indeed.

Closely related to ferns are the horsetails – *Equisetum* spp. (Latin: horse bristle) – a small, world-wide family of twenty species, some twelve of which occur in Britain. According to the fossil record of coal deposits, these plants were once the dominant vegetation of this planet, some of them even reaching tree size. They are among the most ancient of land plants. The stems are of two kinds, fertile and sterile; that is, the fruiting head is present or absent. The fertile heads appear early in the year, shed their spores and wither away. The plant is represented for the rest of the season by the taller green sterile stems which are hollow and segmented. Sheaths are present at the joint of each segment. Whorls of branches, which are also jointed and sheathed, arise from the base of each sheath on the main stem. The horsetails are very distinctive plants.

Above left: In the buckler ferns, the sori (capsules containing the spore-bearing sporangia) are visible as clusters beneath the frond. The membrane shrinks and ruptures and sporangia release the spores. In the photograph, this has happened to the three sori at the end of the leaflet.

Above right: Bracken is the most familiar and widespread of ferns; it is particularly common on acid heathland soils. It grows from extensive underground rhizomes, which are deep in the soil – one reason why it is so difficult to eradicate from land. It can grow in sheltered situations up to 3 m (9–10 ft) high. Spores are

released from sporangia which form a continuous line along the margin of the ultimate segments of the leaf.

Right: Horsetails (Equisetum spp.) are allied to ferns. The great horsetail, shown here, grows in wet woodland, often in the swampy ground around a spring. Horsetails grew like trees in the Carboniferous period. Today they have creeping rhizomes which can exist several feet underground. The fruiting cones (near right) are borne above the surface in early spring. Other sterile stems carry the stiff radiating whorls of leaves later (far right).

Fungi vary from the dusty moulds that grow on bread and other food, and the yeasts used in making wine and beer to the large structures that we loosely call 'mushrooms' and 'toadstools' according to whether we think they are edible or poisonous.

The larger fungi include several which are very poisonous, many which are poisonous enough to make most people unpleasantly ill, some species which apparently are harmless to most people but are not worth eating and several species which are very good to eat – although they have little food value apart from a high vitamin 'D' content in some.

Among the edible species are two or three called mushrooms, but there is a related species, the yellow staining mushroom, which is quite poisonous. The yellow stain appears on the white cap or stem when it is bruised. There is no way of testing a fungus to tell whether it is poisonous or edible other than learning to recognize the characteristics of edible species with absolute certainty. Merely by testing, for example, whether they peel, or turn silver black is not sufficient proof. Even the most poisonous fungus can thus pass as edible and people have died as a result. Salt, vinegar and boiling do not necessarily neutralize the poisons.

The *Amanita* family include three deadly poisonous species. The most frequent cause of death is *Amanita phalloides* – the death-cap. Symptoms do not appear for ten to twelve hours, by which time the several poisons which have not yet been properly identified, or understood, have been absorbed into the body and little can be done to save the victim. Death follows after several days.

Fungi are plants that do not possess chlorophyll – the green substance that enables plants to make starch and sugar from carbon dioxide in the air using sunlight – so they cannot make food and must obtain it elsewhere. Most feed on dead material, usually vegetative, but some are parasitic and grow on living organisms, such as the fungi that kill trees, as well as the microscopic forms that cause skin diseases.

The fungus plant is a mat of filamentous, single-celled threads, called hyphae; the mass of threads that forms a network underground or in wood is called the mycelium. The growth that we regard as a toadstool is the fruiting body that the mycelium has grown through the surface of the ground or the bark of the tree so that the spores of the plant may be released into the air and distributed. Millions are released by one cap. One calculation gives 16,000,000 spores as the product of one average mushroom and another estimate is of seven billion spores from one giant puffball. The 'smoke' emitted from a puffball when touched is a cloud of spores.

The saprophytes (*sapros* means dead, *phyta* means plant) that feed on dead organic matter are a

Plants without Flowers

most important part of the whole pattern of life, for they break down such material chemically and render it available to be reused as part of the chemical constituents of the soil needed by plants.

The importance of fungi in relation to the soil and other plants cannot be over-emphasized. It can be readily observed that certain species of fungi are always found in association with the same trees; for example, the fly agaric with birch trees, the panther cap with beech and a boletus species with larch. Besides the *Boletus* and *Amanita* families, many others, such as the *Russula* spp., the milkcaps (*Lactarius* spp.) and the *Tricholoma* spp. are associated with trees. The mycelium of the fungus grows with a fine mantle around the finer roots of the tree and forms what must be called a fungus-root or mycorrhiza. The mycorrhiza virtually replaces the hair roots of the tree, completely surrounding the root and, in fact, penetrating it. They absorb water for the root and make minerals from the soil available to it. In return, the root supplies the fungus with the sugars that it needs. The importance of this relationship between fungi and trees is not completely understood but it is thought that, to some extent, trees are dependent on fungi for their proper growth and that the fungi will not fruit without the presence of the tree.

The fruiting bodies of fungi take many forms besides the stalked toadstool with its cap. The most common of the other shapes are the 'shelf' and 'bracket' fungi that grow on living or dead trees.

Opposite page (top left): Mushroom is a name that is used rather confusingly – sometimes to describe any edible fungi, as distinct from poisonous toadstools. More correctly, it is used for one group of edible species. The photograph shows the largest, the horse mushroom – it grows to 20 cm/12 in across – which some people prefer to the common field mushroom.

Opposite page (centre): Amanita phalloides – the death cap – is responsible for over 90 per cent of deaths from fungus poisoning; an almost equally high proportion of those who have eaten it have died. Any fungus with a bulbous base to the stem is best regarded as poisonous. Amanita phalloides is recognized by the large cup-like frill (volva) around the base; the colour of this fungus can vary considerably.

Opposite page (bottom): The fly agaric (Amanita muscara), also poisonous, is frequently used in illustrations as it is so attractive in appearance.

Top: Strange and beautiful is the vivid, orange-coloured cup fungus – the orange-peel fungus.

Above: The sulphur polypore is the most striking and colourful of all the bracket fungi. This specimen grew to the size shown of 73 cm (29 in) in width in the space of eight days on an oak tree.

Upper right: One of the few blue fungi is the beautiful, and to some people poisonous, verdigris fungus.

Lower near right: Most strange and interesting is the stinkhorn (Phallus impudicus). It can grow in a few hours. The smell of the cap is very strong and foetid and can be detected from some way away. Its purpose is to attract flies who feed on the dark spore-laden liquid.

Lower far right: The fairyclubs (Clavaria spp.) are delicately shaped. Some are branched like coral; some grow on the ground and others on decaying wood.

Leaflitter & Grassroots Life

A vast microscopic plant population is constantly breaking down, building up and changing both organic and inorganic materials in the soil. But there is also a microscopic animal population that is assisting in the process. Soils are not as solid as they appear – most contain only 50 per cent solid matter while the other 50 per cent of the space is taken up with water and air in the microscopic crevices between the soil particles.

In this water and air, bacteria are teeming together with larger protozoans, sometimes just visible to the naked eye, like amoeba which will feed on the bacteria and the roundworms. Some roundworms, or nematodes, such as eelworms, are so small it might well take fifty of them end to end to make an inch, or twenty to make a centimetre.

There have been many estimates of the quantity of minute animal life in the soil. One calculation of the numbers, in high humus soil, for example, is up to 200,000 to a square metre. Earthworms make up the heaviest and biggest part of the larger animal life in the soil. Earthworms are nocturnal; they do not like heat or light as they breathe through the skin and this must remain moist. They are not as sensitive to red or blue light as they are to white, thus a red-covered torch should be used for night observation of worm behaviour. At night, earthworms emerge almost completely from their burrows to obtain dead organic material – leaves, grass and so on – which they drag down in to the burrow, pointed end first.

In temperate climates, they burrow deeply during the winter until they are lower than the frost level; there, they curl up tightly and hibernate. Earthworms also burrow deeply in hot semi-desert conditions and become dormant.

They are sensitive to vibration and noise. Although some vibrations alarm them so that they retreat underground, other noises attract them and bring them to the surface. This has been observed especially on motorway verges, where vehicles are causing vibration.

An earthworm is little more than a digestive tract separated from another muscular outer tube by a fluid. The outer, segmented tube can 'pump' itself along by muscular pressure on the fluid. Four rows of horny bristles enable a section of its length to grip the ground while the rest moves. The number of rings or segments has nothing to do with the age of the worm and it can only regrow the first few rings at either end of its body. If it is cut in half it will die.

Earthworms are both male and female (hermaphrodite) but the male cells are ready before the female cells and so self-fertilization is not possible. A mutual exchange of male cells between two earthworms occurs and each then holds the other's sperm until it is ready to lay its own eggs in a ring of thick slime from which it slides. The slime hardens and forms a capsule in the soil and the eggs hatch between one and three months later.

The importance of earthworms is often emphasized, and justifiably so. They feed on organic material that has started to rot, but they cannot break it down completely without the aid of vast numbers of bacteria in their digestive systems. This organic paste, highly charged with bacteria, is excreted into the soil (not all species of worms make casts upon the surface). Earthworms constantly excrete small amounts of nitrogen compounds through pores in their skin. Therefore, earthworms perform three major functions: they turn and 'plough' organic matter into the soil; they aerate the soil and prevent fermentation which would sour it. By excretion of broken down organic material and bacteria, they fertilize the soil. Worm casts contain

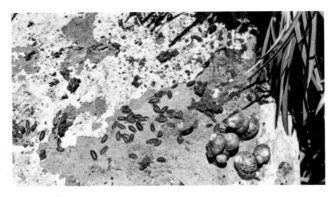

Above: On a hot summer day, snails, woodlice and a black garden slug shelter under a concrete slab. The snail, in periods of dry weather, seals its shell with a waterproof membrane that allows sufficient air to enter. This summer 'hibernation' is called 'aestivation'.

Below: The common garden snail moving across a wall at night. This snail achieves movement by travelling waves of motion across the muscular 'foot'. The slime, which provides a slippery roadway for travelling over rough surfaces, is secreted from a gland at the front of the 'foot'.

Above: A common, large slug – this particular species varies in colour from rich chestnut or orange to dark brown and black. This pearly grey specimen is showing the breathing aperture open and well to the front of the mantle, which identifies the Arion group. The breathing hole is always on the right side of the mantle and there is a pronounced frill around the foot. Sense organs are concentrated at the front, where they are most needed. The small pair of horns, like the upper lip, are used for tasting, whereas the larger pair of horns can function as 'eyes' but are, in fact, capable of little more than detecting light.

Right: Another Arion *or round-backed slug, with a different coloured frill around the foot, is shown in the retracted position. The oval eggs presumably belong to this individual, as they are fresh. Eggs are laid in the autumn but do not hatch until the following spring.*

five times more bacteria than the surrounding soil.

Living close to the soil is another group of animals – the molluscs – a very ancient and successful group. They have survived all over the world for millions of years, having been one of the first forms of animal life to live on land. Slugs and snails are the same kind of animal. They both have a single foot that can travel on a coating of slime and they are both hermaphrodites who need moisture to live. Both have a lung and breathe air and both eat, digest and reproduce in similar ways. Their only difference is that three smaller groups of the land molluscs have, quite separately, evolved without a shell. These are the three groups we call slugs.

There are over fifty species of land snails and twenty species of slugs in Britain but fortunately only a handful of them are harmful. A small group of slugs are carnivorous. They have a remnant of a shell at the rear end of their body and feed on other slugs and worms. The majority of slugs feed on rotting plant material and fungi. The black garden and speckled grey field slugs cause great damage in gardens and are most common between September and December.

Snails have a breathing tube on the right hand side of their body, just under the edge of the shell, which can be seen when they are extended. Slugs have a breathing aperture, just on the edge of the mantel which is the raised hump on the back covering the 'lung'. Both snails and slugs have rasp-like tongues that scrape up food and both are nocturnal feeders as there is great danger to them from dry conditions during the day. They are also adept at avoiding drought and frost.

Slugs and snails are a class – *Gastropoda* or 'belly-foot' – of the large group of *Mollusca* (soft-bodied creatures). There is another vast group of animals also named by their means of locomotion; these are the *Arthropoda* – those with jointed legs – which, besides the mites and springtails, include crabs, spiders, scorpions, woodlice, centipedes, millipedes and the insects. Of all the species of animals in the world ('animals' means birds, fish, insects and reptiles as well as mammals), almost 80 per cent consist of the arthropod species. Like molluscs, many are aquatic, marine or freshwater, but a large number live in the soil or among the natural litter on the surface.

In general, these creatures have segmented bodies, which have been developed in many cases with certain segments fused together. They have eyes, which in the case of insects have been highly developed, and they all have a hard external skeleton or 'shell' skeleton, which cannot grow. This problem is solved in several ways, all of which involve shedding a skin and growing quickly before the new one has hardened. Often there is a special stage, the nymph or larval stage, which is a growing period in the creature's life; when 'adult', the growing stops, after the transformation of pupating – the 'chrysalis' period. In other creatures, such as the crabs and

spiders, moulting of the skin occurs all through the growing time and stops when full size is reached; this is without any fundamental change of shape or 'life-style'.

Soil creatures generally have adapted to conditions of darkness, dampness and cool temperatures. Like the snails and slugs, many of them are nocturnal; they spend the daytime sheltering from sun, wind and enemies under leaves, stones, rocks and logs. Woodlice are often found where slugs and snails occur, because they too require humidity – not dryness. They are related to crabs, lobsters and shrimps (crustacea) and feed mostly on decaying vegetation.

Their hard, armoured covering is not waterproof and desiccation is a major danger; humid conditions are essential. They grow slowly and are not mature until two years old. The female carries the eggs around in a brood pouch under her body. Although all species have 'jointed armourplates' that allow movement, only one, the pill-wood louse, can curl up into a ball. This particular creature can be confused with the pill millipede, which can behave in a similar way but they can easily be distinguished by counting their legs.

Millipedes are largely vegetarian, too. Most of them curl up when disturbed but in a coil like a snake

Opposite page: This cockchafer or May-bug is the adult beetle of the white grub. The adult feeds on the foliage of trees, but is usually noticed when it flies in through windows at night.

Top left: Oniscus *spp. are some of the most common woodlice.*

Top right: Pill millipedes are often confused with pill wood-lice which have only seven pairs of legs while the millipede has seventeen pairs (female) and nineteen pairs (male).

Above left: The flatbacked

millipede – Polydesmus com-planatus *– is common in de-ciduous woodland.*

Above right: Centipedes are easily distinguished from milli-pedes. At first glance they are quick moving predators; a second glance shows they have one pair of legs per segment of the body whereas millipedes have two.

Below: Climbing up a stem of grass, this snake millipede is demonstrating the waves of leg movement by which the creature travels about.

rather than a ball – hence the name for the hard, smooth species of 'snake-millipedes'. As a further means of defence, they have 'stink-glands' along the sides of the body, which make them distasteful to enemies. They have a varied number of legs accord-ing to species, but there are consistently two pairs of legs per body segment (except the first two) and not one pair as in centipedes. Like most vegetarians in the world of small creatures, they are comparatively slow movers. Millipedes are common inhabitants of the leaf-litter in woodland.

Centipedes, however, being carnivorous and having poison fangs, are very fast moving. Some tropical species can inflict a poisonous bite. They do not have 100 legs but the number varies from species to species, like millipedes. Millipedes increase the number of segments and pairs of legs each time they shed a skin (ecdysis) and one common group of centipedes (*Lithobiomorpha* spp. – 'stone-dwellers') do the same: they start with seven pairs and end up with fifteen pairs. This same group of centipedes lay their eggs individually, disguised with soil. Other centipedes lay their eggs in batches; these batches and the resultant young are attended by the female. Millipedes lay their eggs in a little nest made of soil and excrement. Fertilization in centipedes is indirect; the male deposits a small bag of sperm (spermatophore) which the female then takes into her body.

Along with the shield plant-bugs or stink-bugs, some centipedes, and social insects like ants, wasps and bees, the earwig has the distinction of being an invertebrate animal that guards and looks after its young. It, too, lays batches of up to fifty eggs in a cavity in the soil. Eggs and young of creatures inhabiting the soil are liable to attack from moulds; one of the reasons the mother earwig stays 'on guard' is periodically to clean them and to protect them from fungal attack. Earwigs hatch as miniatures of the parents, but without the adult wings; these begin to develop and grow with each moult (ecdysis). Although they do eat some vegetable material, as all those gardeners who grow dahlias well know, they are mainly predatory upon other invertebrates in the leaf-litter.

The two major pests in the soil are probably leather jackets, which are the larvae of the crane-fly, sometimes confusingly called 'daddy-long-legs' (as is another creature) and wireworms, which are the larvae of the click beetle or 'skip-jack' – if it should find itself lying on its back, it can, by a 'trigger' device, flick itself into the air and turn right over. A third soil pest is the larva of the cockchafer beetle, or maybug, which is sometimes called the 'white grub'. The adult beetle – which often flies into lighted rooms at night – feeds on the leaves of trees.

Spiders are an important group of predatory hunters on the ground as well as builders of webs in the grass, plants and bushes. There are some spiders that build webs on or near the ground. One of the most noticeable, perhaps on the bank of a hedgerow, is the flat platform of the 'funnel-web' spider. The spread of silk tapers away to the funnel-shaped entrance of a tube. The spider waits in the tube and immediately comes out when the web vibrates from the struggles of a victim caught in the surface of the web. The common house spider is a close relative.

There are other spiders who suspend tensioned threads from a platform to the ground. When a victim, such as an ant, is caught by a globule of glue on the thread and, in its struggles, breaks the thread, the tension jerks the ant off its feet and the spider hauls it up and administers a poisonous bite. Still other spiders spread a simple web on the ground and wait in a crack or cavity below.

There are, however, several kinds of spiders that do not build webs as snares. Among these are the active little jumping spiders that can leap on to their prey. There are also the crab spiders that lie in wait in a camouflaged situation. But most common are the little wolf spiders (*Lycosidae*) who, like a similar hunting spider of the grassland (*Pisaura* spp.), chase and pounce on their victims.

Both the wolf spider (*Lycosa* spp.) and *Pisaura* carry their eggs in a capsule. *Pisaura* is unusual because the male makes a present of a wrapped-up fly to occupy the female's attention whilst he mates with her. A species of crab spider ties the female down with silk before mating. The act of mating is in

spiders exceptional. Apart from the elaborate courtship dances that many males must indulge in to ensure the female has 'got the message', the male spiders have a specially adapted pair of palps, like two boxing gloves, extending from the front of the head. In these receptacles he places his sperm, ready to insert into the female. As she is usually larger and dangerous, this device allows him to function from a safer distance.

Spiders usually have eight eyes arranged in various patterns, according to the species, in the front and on top of the head. All have fangs with which they deliver venom into their victims, but only a few are large enough to harm humans and only one of these, the black widow spider, is really dangerous. Their bite is very painful and has been known to cause death. There are several species in southern Europe, the Near East, Africa, southern Asia, Australia, South America and North America.

Related to spiders are scorpions, pseudo scorpions, whip scorpions and wind scorpions or sun spiders. Most occur only in hot, dry climates. Of the 700 species of scorpion in the world at least twenty or thirty species occur in America. Pseudo scorpions are tiny (less than 5 mm), harmless inhabitants of leaf-litter which occur commonly everywhere.

Related to spiders and also common are harvestmen or 'daddy-long-legs'. However, they differ from spiders by the fact that their body consists of one fused unit. They are nocturnal and carnivorous and have two eyes usually set on a small hummock.

It is not possible to look at creatures inhabiting the ground of garden, woodland or field without

Opposite page: The garden black ant is the most familiar ant in urban areas, as it nests under paving stones and concrete slabs. The winged queens and males are noticeable when they are about to make their mating flights. Worker ants do not have wings. They are predators and scavengers and, apart from entering houses and attacking fruit, they are never harmful to man.

Above: The dainty Pisaura is another common wolf spider which hunts on the ground. She also carries an egg capsule around but held under the front of her body by her jaws. She will build a cocoon in the grass ready for the young when they hatch. Look for her in the summer from mid June to July.

Top right: A female wolf spider (Lycosa spp.) has carried her eggs in a capsule attached to her spinnerets for a week or two; now they have emerged and have climbed onto her abdomen where they will be carried for several days. This sight is common in July on the woodland floor or hedgerow bank.

Centre left: A close-up view of the spinnerets of a woodland relative of the garden spider, showing the hind legs drawing the silk from the spinnerets. The silk in the spider's body is a thick liquid that has to be 'dragged' out, changing its character in

the process, retaining an elasticity but acquiring very great strength.

Centre right: A sun-spider or wind scorpion is a near relation of spiders. Species are found in most warm, dry countries. It has no venomous fangs but probably the biggest and most fearsome jaws in the invertebrate world. It can reduce a 5 cm (2 in) grasshopper into a small bundle of chewed bits in less than a minute.

Bottom left: This is Dolomedes fimbriatus – or the raft spider as it is erroneously called. The error arose from a mistaken observation that it made a raft of leaves to float upon. A better name would be swamp spider. It is the largest spider in Britain, the body measuring up to 20 mm (0·79 in). This spider is found beside still lakes and pools. The egg capsule is carried in its jaws for 2–3 weeks before a sheltering cocoon is built in vegetation ready for the young to emerge.

Bottom right: One of our most familiar spiders is the garden cross spider, so named after the marking on top of the abdomen. This is the spider seen so often in the centre of its web during the latter part of the summer. The female in the photograph has caught a large fly in her web and has bitten and enshrouded it in silk before she decides to suck out the liquid parts.

seeing ants. Ants are insects and live in a social organization. Most of the 'worker' ants have no wings; the winged specimens are males and females (queens); the females are large. When weather conditions are suitable (still and warm) the queens leave the nests, followed by the males, to indulge in the nuptial flight. The females return to the ground after mating and start new nests.

Ants are largely predators upon other insects and, in this sense, are beneficial to man. Wood ants' nests are protected in the forests of Germany because they are considered valuable as predators assisting in the control of pest insects. Some species regularly augment their carnivorous diet by becoming 'pastoralists' and 'milking' colonies of aphids to obtain the surplus sugar that the aphids excrete.

Wasps and many beetles, ground beetles and rove beetles are also carnivorous hunters among the leaf-litter and the grass-roots. Birds are the major predators, although the larger animals, frogs and toads, mice, moles, hedgehogs and foxes and badgers also consume the larger soil invertebrates.

Amphibians and Reptiles

Distaste and revulsion are common reactions to these harmless creatures, which are really among the greatest friends of man the gardener. The group of creatures we call amphibians – frogs, toads and newts – will eat almost any creature of the right size that they find moving at ground level in the vegetation of a garden. A giant toad, up to 22·5 cm (8·86 in), has been deliberately introduced in to the sugar cane plantations of the West Indies and other parts of the world because of its appetite for insects.

Amphibians are the smallest group of vertebrates (backboned animals) in the world. There are some 2,500 different species, which vary from a little known group of nearly blind, burrowing, worm-like creatures called Caecilians to the giant salamanders of China and Japan which grow up to 1·5–2 m (5–6 ft) in length. The two main groups are frogs and toads, and newts and salamanders.

Although the breeding cycle of one amphibian – the frog, of which there are 1,800 species – is well known to almost every schoolchild, there are mysterious aspects of its behaviour of which we know little and mysterious facts about its physiology which we still cannot explain properly.

Modern amphibians are the remaining descend-

Above left: The common toad does not hop or leap like a frog but usually crawls comparatively slowly. The toad's skin is dryer and the 'pimples' (or glands) are more noticeable than in the frog. Note the eyes and nostrils high on the head.

Above right: The common frog – known as the grass frog in Germany and the red frog in France – has a moister, smoother skin than the toad. Its hind legs, with which it leaps, are much longer, too. Urban development and water pollution are contributing to its decline in Britain. In Holland, efforts are being made to protect the frog and it is illegal to take the spawn or tadpoles from ponds.

Below: In spring the male common newt becomes dark and develops a wavy crest down his back. This individual, photographed in July, has finished breeding; his crest is disappearing and he is pale. Soon he will leave the pond and will not return until the spring of the following year.

Above: Very strange behaviour – and quite futile, too! Because there was a shortage of female frogs – possibly caused by over-collecting by children, parents, teachers or pet-shop owners – this male common frog seized a female toad as a substitute. Inter-breeding between the two species is completely unknown. In both frogs and toads, the male clings to the back of the female during mating. This coupled position is called 'amplexus'.

Right: Instinctive behaviour gone berserk! Eight male toads cling to one unfortunate female whose legs can be seen at the top of the picture. Seven males were removed to another part of the pond. The behaviour was caused by a shortage of females.

Below: Amplexus, the instinctive behaviour of a male common toad who clings to the female until she has finished laying her eggs.

ants of the creatures that were once the most advanced form of life on Earth. Life began in the oceans and moved to the land, initially in plant form. This made it possible for vegetarian animals to leave the water. Some fish developed lungs and so could use the oxygen in the air. Their pectoral fins developed and these were used as a means of dragging themselves out of the water, as in the case of the modern mudskipper fish.

In time, these fish became 'amphibians'. This very gradual change took a long time and merely to rename them as 'amphibians' gives a false impression. The new land creatures – some of which became giants compared with their modern descendants – returned to their original environment to breed. They had adapted their bodies to live on land but the kinder conditions of water were more suitable for breeding. The name amphibia, from the Greek words *amphi* meaning 'both' and *bios* meaning 'life,' describes the ability to live in both aquatic and terrestrial environments. Amphibia are really midway between reptiles and fishes.

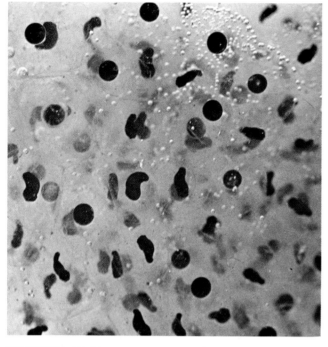

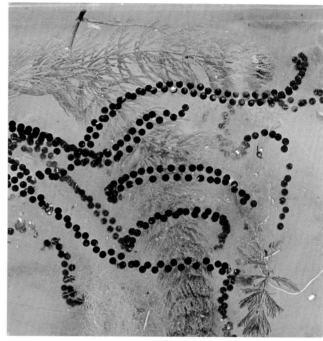

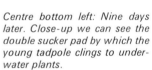

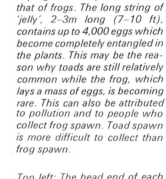

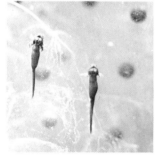

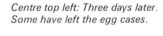

Top right: Toad spawn is unlike that of frogs. The long string of 'jelly', 2–3m long (7–10 ft), contains up to 4,000 eggs which become completely entangled in the plants. This may be the reason why toads are still relatively common while the frog, which lays a mass of eggs, is becoming rare. This can also be attributed to pollution and to people who collect frog spawn. Toad spawn is more difficult to collect than frog spawn.

Top left: The head end of each tadpole can already be distinguished from the tail in this close-up picture.

Centre top left: Three days later. Some have left the egg cases.

Centre top right: Five days later. Almost all have left but they will remain resting for a day or two.

Centre bottom left: Nine days later. Close-up we can see the double sucker pad by which the young tadpole clings to underwater plants.

Centre bottom right: The more familiar tadpole shape is shown here. The rate of growth and development depends upon the temperature.

Bottom left: The legs are developed, the tail is being absorbed and he needs air in his lungs. He starts to look like a frog.

Bottom right: One of the mysteries for which there is no satisfactory explanation is the way in which the tadpole population will swim in a 'disciplined' stream in a clockwise direction round a pond. Experts wonder whether it could be related to the supply of oxygen in the water?

Above: We assume that the same ponds are used, as far as possible, by the same individuals. It seems likely that most frogs will return to the pond in which they were spawned. The consistency of this frog is demonstrated by the result of an accident. It had lost its left foot and thus was easily identifiable. During five consecutive summers it inhabited the same rockery garden 50 m (55 yd) from the nearest pond.

Reproduction The reproductive processes in amphibia are very similar to those in fish. In most cases the eggs are laid and fertilized in the water but there are variations. In frogs and toads, the male clings tenaciously to the female's back to ensure that he is in the right place to fertilize the eggs when they are laid. In most species, he has developed some form of aid to maintain his grip.

The female develops thousands of eggs which, as they pass out of her body, are coated with mucus. The mucus absorbs water and the eggs swell to many times their original size.

In newts and salamanders, mating is a more delicate procedure – not a single, grabbing, embrace as with frogs and toads. The initial courtship manoeuvres of the male usually involve violent, sinuous and wavy movements and nudgings which end directly in front of the female. When the female seems receptive, the male deposits a small mucus bag of sperm in front of the female, who moves into position above it and fertilizes the eggs internally.

Newts and salamanders provide better protection for their eggs than do frogs or toads, and therefore they do not lay so many. Usually the eggs are laid singly on leaves and then folded over with the hindfeet. The female European salamander retains the eggs until they hatch inside her and the live young emerge from her body.

The tadpoles develop differently too. The young newt starts to develop all the adult organs in the egg. The frog or toad tadpole, however, goes through a complete metamorphosis before becoming adult.

Did you know that...

Amphibians do not drink water. Water is absorbed through glands in the skin.

Frogs' optic nerves are 'excited' more by the reception of blue light than any other colour and they move towards it. Possibly this assists them in leaping into water or through holes in a canopy of low vegetation.

Amphibians can change skin colour according to their surroundings over a period of an hour or two. This is achieved by pigment variation at three different levels in the skin. There is also varying light absorption of different colours and thus some colours are reflected. Lightening and darkening is controlled by the amount of secretion of the pigment 'melanin' in the lowest skin layer.

South American Indians use a poison secreted by the giant toad with which to tip their arrows.

The greenbottle fly is parasitic upon the common toad and lays its eggs on the toad's legs. Upon hatching, the larvae make their way rapidly over the skin and enter the nostrils or eyes. The unfortunate toad is asphyxiated and dies within three days.

Late hatching tadpoles will occasionally over-winter in the pond if their development has been too slow to enable them to change in time to hibernate.

Above left: A high population of three-spined sticklebacks in a pond will prevent many newly hatched tadpoles from growing up. This photograph shows the 'redthroat', as the male in courtship colours is called. In the breeding season, his head and back are irridescent and his belly turns a shade of red.

Above right: Enemies of the frog are numerous and mortality is very high among tadpoles. The nymph (larva) of a large dragonfly is a ferocious creature to meet beneath the surface of a pond. The one shown in this photograph is devouring a stickleback. Nymphs have powerful hinged jaws to catch their prey.

Below left: This common toad is reacting to the camera the way in which it would behave in the presence of a snake or similar enemy. It has raised its body on stiffened limbs in an endeavour to appear as large as possible so as to frighten its attacker.

Below right: The great-crested or warty newt, showing the mucus glands, or 'warts', which secrete a poisonous defensive fluid that can cause predators to drop the newt soon after taking it into their mouths, and to show considerable distress and even convulsions. During the mating period, the dorsal crest becomes prominent.

Breathing and feeding In the course of their development from fish to land living animals, the amphibians made other adaptations. Perhaps one of the most important of these is the use of the skin as an organ of respiration.

The skin is as essential a part of 'breathing', even on land, as are the lungs, for respiration through the lungs alone is not enough to support life on land for long. To enable respiration through the skin to occur, the skin must be kept moist. There are mucus secreting glands distributed about the body which facilitate this need.

In water and especially during hibernation, which in many species is in the water and mud at the bottom of a pond, the absorption of oxygen through the skin is the only form of respiration when the metabolism of the body is slowed down to a minimum by the lowered temperature.

When the lungs are in use – and this varies, being most frequent in the breeding season – air is inhaled through the nostrils but, since amphibia have no ribs, the raising and lowering of the floor of the mouth sucks the air in and the contraction of the throat then forces air into the lungs.

The amphibian's food – prey – must move before it will eat it, and thus sight is a dominant sense. However, in newts and salamanders there is some sense of smell since they can detect and locate pieces of meat. Frogs and toads apparently have no sense of smell. While newts and salamanders snap at their prey, the tail-less amphibians have developed a tongue that is attached at the front of the lower jaw and which can lengthen and project itself out from the mouth, in some cases almost as far as a third of the body length. The complete flick in and out of the tongue takes little more than one tenth of a second.

When a frog or toad swallows, the eyes are shut. This occurs because the eyeballs are withdrawn downwards and used to squash the food against the bottom of the mouth. A salivary gland – the paratoid – is noticeable behind the eye of some amphibians. In the common toad it is prominent and sausage-shaped but in some species this has developed as a poison gland. Poison glands have also evolved in the skin – the large 'warts' on the back of the common toad, for example. The poison is used as a defence and produces quite a violent reaction in the mouth of a predator.

Apparently – according to one scientist who has tested this personally – the effects are burning and smarting, numbness, foaming, inflammation, fever and headache and limb pains. These symptoms have been observed in dogs and cats, together with convulsions and considerable distress. However, death has not been recorded.

Keeping amphibians and reptiles

Amphibians and some reptiles make interesting creatures to keep and observe. Generally speaking, the reptiles must avoid being constantly wet or else they cannot slough (shed) their skins properly and so develop skin infections. A reptile's skin should be dry and silky to touch. Amphibians, on the other hand, will perish if kept in a very dry habitat. An old aquarium that leaks can be converted to a vivarium.

The damp vivarium should be filled with up to 5 cm (2 in) of loam in which a shallow bowl or dish of water should be sunk. Mosses and most common house plants can be planted. The cover should be glass, raised slightly for ventilation by match-sticks to create a sufficiently humid atmosphere. A low wattage bulb above the glass can provide light and a certain amount of warmth. Rocks, stones or bark can be arranged to provide hiding places. The amount of food will vary according to the size of the creature but generally soil animals, such as slugs, snails, worms, beetles and woodlice, are suitable. Very small amphibians will eat aphids on a shoot.

Breeding aquarium: In the breeding season amphibians should be transferred to a normal water-filled aquarium. Add some pond water to provide the necessary microscopic life, and an inch or two of aquarium gravel on the bottom. Provide a thicket of plants and some rocks that project above the surface. Place the aquarium (before filling) on a light window sill, away from direct sunlight. Like the vivarium, cover with glass. Remove adults after spawning. Microscopic plant food (algae) is necessary for the first few weeks of tadpole life, then provide minute animal food caught with a fine net. Use small pieces of raw meat, suspended on cotton for easy removal, but beware of polluting the water. Clean the bottom and renew most of the water if it turns cloudy (other than green) and reduce the amount of food.

As the young try to crawl out, remove them to the damp vivarium or release them. Do not place them in with the adults or they will quickly disappear.

The dry vivarium for snakes and lizards should be provided with at least 5 cm (2 in) of dry sandy soil or peat. Plants are not necessary and a small drinking bowl should be sunk in the soil. Caverns should be provided under flat stones or a large piece of bark. Rocks or stones can be used to confine an area of dry grass, bracken or sphagnum moss and also to provide a warm sunning spot.

The vivarium should be well ventilated with a cover of perforated zinc or similar fine mesh covering. Remember, a snake can lift a badly fitting cover with its head surprisingly easily. A low wattage bulb let into the cover will provide an artificial sun and necessary warmth. Sunlight can be used but beware of over-heating.

During the winter, choose a frost-free place – such as a cellar – where the temperature will remain low until the spring. If hibernation is not intended, they must be kept warm and fed.

Top: The yellow and black collar and long slender shape distinguish the harmless grass snake, seen in the picture, from the adder. In Europe, it is called the barred grass snake, to distinguish it from the grass or ringed snake, a related species which does not occur in Britain.

Above and below: The adder or northern viper is probably the most common snake in Britain.

The dark zigzag line is the obvious marking that identifies the adder though it is not always as clear as this. The body is thicker and the tail shorter than in the grass snake. Although the adder's mouth is closed, the triangular opening, out of which the tongue can dart, is visible. Although the adder's bite is fatal to smaller mammals, it seldom is for humans. Only seven deaths have been recorded in 50 years.

Reptiles   To the revulsion commonly felt for the amphibians, we must add horror and fear to describe many people's reaction to snakes and reptiles. But most of the snakes and reptiles that can harm us will usually only do so in self defence.

There are more than 7,000 species of reptile in the world, 2,500 of which are species of snake. Others are lizards, crocodiles, alligators, turtles and tortoises. The giant tortoise is said to live for 150 years. In the past, reptiles included the largest and fiercest creatures that have ever walked our planet – the brontosaurus and tyrannosaurus.

Reptiles exist in greatest numbers in warm or hot climates, where they also tend to grow larger than they do elsewhere. The largest snakes are the anacondas of South America and the pythons of South East Asia, both of which reach a length of more than ten metres (30 feet). Some reptiles, however, such as the adder and the common or viviparous lizard, can survive right up to the Arctic Circle.

Being 'cold blooded' means that the reptiles' temperature will always be similar to their surroundings. Thus, in Europe and North America, hibernation is necessary during the winter. In the far north, the hibernation of the adder can be as long as eight or nine months. In these latitudes the breeding cycle cannot be completed in one year, and fertilization and birth take place in consecutive years.

In two major ways, reptiles have developed further than amphibians towards living on land ('terrestrial life'). They have developed a scaly skin which protects them from desiccation and they have adapted their reproduction to land by laying eggs which have a soft fibrous shell. Some have taken this adaptation further: the female retains the eggs in her body until they hatch.

Lizards   Most lizards have legs, but snakes and one lizard (the slow worm) no longer have limbs. There are other minor differences, too. Snakes have developed a fixed covering over their eyes and, unlike lizards, they do not have eyelids. They also have no external ear and their jawbones are especially adapted, as is their elongated shape.

Possibly the most unique and well-known adaptation possessed by most lizards (and the slow worm) is their ability to deliberately shed their tail as a defensive manoeuvre. When in danger and seized by the tail, the lizard (and slow worm) can cause its bone to part along an existing fracture line. It does this by contracting the muscle at a point in a vertebra above which it is being held by the predator. The tail remains behind, twitching and contorting with nerve reflexes which distract the predator while the lizard escapes.

Above and right: In these pictures a common lizard and a grass snake are shedding the outer layer of their skin. The frequency with which this occurs varies. It can be three or four times a year or as often as once a month. The removal is assisted by the animal rubbing itself against rough surfaces. It is essential that they shed their skins to permit body growth.

Below: This close-up of a common lizard is deceptively large. It shows the large hindfeet used in climbing and the scales of the skin.

Above left: The slow worm is a lizard that has dispensed with the need for legs. The three slow worms shown in this photograph clearly indicate the variations in colour. They are widespread in northern, central and western Europe, including Britain.

Above right: The slow worm is well named – but then why move fast when your favourite food is slugs and worms? Slugs are seized from above and across the middle and although the vic-tim will exude so much slime that the slow worm's face is almost covered it will be to no avail – the slow worm will eat him regardless and merely wipe his face on the ground when the meal is finished.

Below: A grass snake with its mouth closed but its forked, scent tasting tongue is constantly sampling the air. Grass snakes eat worms and slugs and also small mammals such as voles and mice. They are often found near water.

The lizard's feet are extremely efficient as a means of climbing and running at high speed, and also in obtaining 'claw holds' on rocks apparently in defiance of gravity. The wall lizard is especially skilled in this.

Lizards, like snakes, have a need periodically to cast off the outer layer of their skin. The lizard's skin comes away in pieces but in the snake it is usually shed or 'sloughed' in one piece. Snakes are also different in that they have no eyelids. The eye is covered with a transparent scale which is shed, intact, with the skin.

Snake jaws Snakes do not have external ears and it is certain that they cannot 'hear' in the normally accepted sense, although this does not mean they are unaware of 'sounds'. Normal ear structure, as possessed by other animals, does not exist but a rod of bone is attached to the moving hinge bone of the jaw. We do not know how this functions but one might assume that, since they are certainly aware of sounds such as footsteps, the sense involved is one of detecting sound through the ground and bone in some way.

Its jaw is a wonderful adaptation to the snake's need to pass through small holes and yet be able to swallow large meals whole.

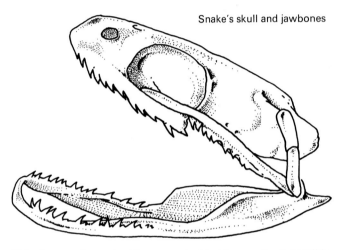

Snake's skull and jawbones

This diagram shows the hinge-effect of the snake's jaw. Freely moving jaw-bones and a double hinge make it possible for a snake to swallow prey larger than its head.

The bones of the jaws – the upper jaw, the hinge bones and the lower jaw – are loosely attached to the skull and can move independently. But what is unique is the snake's ability to move both upper right and upper left jaws separately, and to do the same with the lower jaws which are linked at the front with cartilage. Thus, by the hinge swinging the lower jaw bone forward, the gape is extremely wide; by moving left and right separately in a chewing action, the grip on the prey is not released while swallowing proceeds. The mouth of the windpipe – the glottis – is in the front of the floor of the mouth and can be pushed forward to enable the snake to breathe while swallowing.

In the poisonous vipers and cobras, the long, hollow fangs, through which venom is injected into the wound, are hinged and only loosely linked with ducts leading to the venom gland above the roof of the mouth. Replacement fangs are always available in reserve should damage or loss occur.

The snake probably has little sense of taste but it has a highly developed sense of smell in which the tongue plays a major part. The tongue has a forked tip and, being 'stored' in a tube in the bottom of the snake's mouth, does not interfere when large prey are swallowed. A small opening in the 'lips' allows the tongue to pass in and out without the necessity of opening the jaws. The role of the tongue is essentially one of constantly tasting the scent particles in the air and conveying them to a pair of specialized chambers in the roof of the mouth known as 'Jacobson's organs'.

Are they poisonous?

In Europe, there are no lizards that are dangerous to man. The only venomous reptiles in Europe are the adders or vipers, and of the four species only two – the Aspic viper (France, Switzerland, Italy and the Pyrenees) and the horned, or sand viper (Russia, the Balkans and the Tyrol), are highly dangerous. Bites from the northern adder and the field adder are not necessarily fatal. All other European snakes are harmless. In North America there are several venomous snakes besides the well-known rattlesnake and one poisonous lizard.

The adders or vipers are easily recognized by their comparatively short, thick bodies which narrow abruptly to the tail. They all have a wavy or zigzag dark line down the back which is usually well marked. Any snake that is too dark to distinguish a line, should also be avoided since dark or melanistic forms of the adder are not uncommon.

It is wise to avoid handling any snake which is unidentified. To catch or remove a snake, without handling it, try placing a bag or even a rubber boot in front of the creature – they tend to crawl into dark cavities. If it is really necessary to handle an adder, then wear thick gloves and pick it up by the tail when the body is extended.

Treatment for a bite is (a) avoid panic, calm the victim, and (b) seek medical advice as soon as possible.

Modern treatment in Britain, where only the northern adder is found, is only to give serum if the symptoms are severe.

In one respect lizards and snakes have a pair of organs where most other creatures have only one. The male snake or lizard has a pair of sex organs, which are internally stored when not required but which can be protruded when erect from either side of the body and are normally used one at a time. Fertilization occurs internally and, because of hook-like horns on the male organ, coupling usually is a prolonged affair.

With certain exceptions, most lizards and snakes lay clusters of soft shelled eggs. The lizards lay in holes, hollows and sometimes beneath stones but the snakes frequently cover their eggs with piles of rotting vegetation where the extra heat assists incubation.

The exceptions are the viviparous (or common) lizard, the slow worm and the adders or vipers, plus the third snake to be found in Britain, the smooth snake. This snake is now particularly rare and only lives in a handful of very specialized areas. They are exceptional in that they retain the eggs inside the female until they hatch or are about to hatch – the female then 'gives birth' to a litter of live miniatures of herself.

The grass snake, although harmless, has several methods of defence. If surprised in the open, it will coil up, hiss and strike with closed mouth. If picked up, it may do three things: it may go limp, open its mouth and feign death or, if it has recently eaten, disgorge its dead or, sometimes, still living last meal. What it is most certain to do, and which is most unpleasant, is to discharge from its anal gland a milky fluid which has the most vile smell imaginable. This has great value in disgusting a would-be attacker and is also probably used in territorial and sexual behaviour.

Top left, bottom left and above: The action in this series of photographs took place in the space of two or three minutes. Once the frog moved, the snake seized it by a hindfoot and its fate was decided. The frog held a rigid posture until, too late, it began to struggle. Its only hope had been, by its rigidity, to persuade the snake that it was either too big to swallow or was not a living creature. The frog is the main source of food of the grass snake and although a meal of this size should be sufficient for several days, a snake has been found with as many as nine medium sized frogs in it. There are also several incidents recorded of living prey being recovered from a snake's gullet where they have existed, unharmed, for several hours.

Watching snakes

Many people have never seen a snake in the wild. How should you go about it?

Snakes are usually very local – thus there are places where you are much more likely to see them.

Some species like warm, dry situations – sunny banks and sheltered clearings among heather and rocks. Others, especially when hunting, may be found in damp or wet areas.

The time of day is important – few will be seen in the full heat of a summer day. Early morning and late afternoon or evening are the best times. Spring is the time of year when they are most active.

How you move is probably even more important! Move very slowly, a few feet at a time. Put your feet down gently and quietly. Stand still for several minutes, searching with your eyes before moving on. Repeat these tactics throughout an area.

Use your ears. A slow continuous rustling in the undergrowth is quite distinct. When it stops, wait, keeping perfectly still.

Watch rather than touch – it is safer and you will probably see more.

Wear sensible shoes and leg coverings (thick socks and trousers). Binoculars are useful.

Do not be disappointed if you fail to see any snakes – you will undoubtedly see a great deal of other interesting things. Good luck!

when should we interfere?

Young animals One of the greatest dangers to young creatures in suburban gardens is the misplaced sentimentality of human beings. A typical example of this behaviour is the occasion when a young song thrush, found by a kind lady who 'could not see its mother anywhere', was fed indoors for two days before advice was sought. *She should have left it alone.* The parent bird was probably somewhere nearby.

It was necessary to feed the young bird for several days and, when it was able to feed itself, food was placed for it in an aviary for two or three weeks until it had become wild enough to be released without flying to humans. Even then, it tended to have no fear of cats and had to be frightened away from food every time a cat approached.

Different problems arise when the creature involved is capable of defending itself more effectively. For example a young rook was taken as a pet by a schoolboy and then released in a suburban neighbourhood when the boy's parents would tolerate no more household damage, mess and thievery. The bird became a local menace; pecking out cement as fast as bricklayers could lay the bricks, stealing from the butcher boy's basket, and finally attacking the nylon-clad legs and ankles of local shoppers. Eventually he had to be recaptured and released far away in open countryside – another example of what happens when a creature is disorientated and loses its natural fear of humans.

Interference in the affairs of young birds is usually an act of cruelty which can only be corrected with great care and inconvenience and sometimes considerable dangers. Almost invariably they are *not* 'lost'. It is only when they are 'taken home to be cared for' that they are lost and then they frequently die from incorrect feeding or, later, from the result of confused instincts.

There are dangers, too, for young mammals from well-meaning human beings. They should never be stroked and petted or the resulting human scent will create a barrier of suspicion between the young creature and its mother.

Fox cubs are attractive, furry animals to humans but as pets they quickly become smelly young foxes with (by human standards) 'vicious' instincts and dirty habits. Later, if they are released, they become 'crazy mixed-up foxes' with no natural 'fear' of man and they are a danger to themselves and to man and his domestic animals and pets.

In spring, young squirrels are frequently found and taken into custody, when they should be left for the mother to reclaim. If their eyes are open they are over five weeks old and could, by their sixth or seventh week, be searching for solid food and exploring their world. Squirrels can be reared from a young age but problems arise when they are older for then they become more destructive and inclined to test things by biting – including fingers, arms, necks. In Britain, a licence is required to rear them.

Above left and right: Month old fox cubs make attractive 'pets' however, they are not so desir- *able three months later when they can be messy, smelly and destructive. It is far better to* *leave them in the wild to explore the woods in the early morning sunshine like this young cub* *During the first few weeks after birth the cubs' almost black fur gradually lightens.*

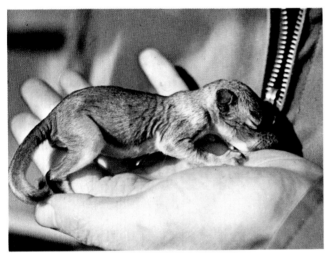

Opposite page: The rook's bill was not fully grown but horrifyingly dangerous as he sat on the side of a pram.

Above: This helpless young squirrel (two weeks old) unfortunately developed enteritis and died.

Below: Another squirrel, already five weeks old in this photograph, was reared successfully.

Right: Now seven weeks old, the squirrel is almost independent and very active. Note that squirrels have five toes on the hindfoot and four on the front foot.

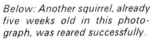

Top left: With their eyes still closed these young hedgehogs, only a few days after birth, are growing a second coat of dark spines among the white spines of the first coat. The new spines will be soft at first.

Centre left: Milk, a favourite bait to encourage regular visits from hedgehogs, is here being lapped up eagerly by a family of juveniles.

Bottom left: Fleas on a hedge-hog normally avoid the light,

staying on hidden parts of the creature. In this photograph, however, a flea is moving down the hedgehog's nose.

Opposite page, near right: A juvenile wood mouse, greyer in colour than an adult, makes a good pet but inevitably involves a health risk.

Opposite page, far right: Tawny owls seem to be frequent victims of poisoning — possibly from insecticides or from eating poisoned and dying rats or mice.

Hedgehogs frequently live near human habitation. Consequently, 'abandoned' young, in or out of a nest, are sometimes found. Often this occurs when the mother is in the midst of moving them to the safety of a second nest after some disturbance has occurred at the first. Hedgehogs will frequently move the whole family, one at a time, usually by the scruff of the neck.

Unless it is certain that the mother is dead, it is best to leave the foundlings alone. However, should human interference become necessary, like all such foster-parentage, a great deal of time and care is required and, even then, success is only likely if the young orphans are considerably older than those in the picture on this page.

Hedgehogs are worth encouraging in the garden for, although they may have a 'sweet tooth' when

offered cake, biscuits or chocolate, their main food consists of creatures found among the natural debris of leaves lying on the ground – slugs, snails, worms, millipedes, beetles and other insects. It is probably more accurate to describe them as omnivorous or insectivorous, as they are known to eat windfallen fruit, table scraps and fruit juices when offered.

Hedgehogs are notorious for carrying a large flea population but they probably carry no more than any other wild mammal; it is just that the fleas are more clearly seen on the hedgehog than on animals with a thicker fur. Fleas are rather fussy and usually prefer their natural host. If you acquire any, they are unlikely to stay long.

It is wise to take precautions and remove fleas from any household pets, using flea powder, as fleas can carry skin infections.

For a more serious reason, it is wise not to encourage children to make pets of wild mice and voles since there is always a risk of becoming infected by a bacterium called leptospirosis – known by several names, one of which is 'sewerman's fever'. This disease is no longer fatal, as it once was, but it is still a serious risk to take.

What to do about orphans, the injured and the sick The first thing we slow-moving human beings should realize is that if we catch, find or pick up a creature that normally will not let us get near, then there is something seriously wrong with it.

The second point to accept is that there is probably little that we can do to solve the problem and thus we must, if we wish to help the creature, accept a third proposition: it may be necessary that the creature is spared further misery by providing a quick death.

If experts are not available, *you* must provide a solution. It is usually not difficult to acccomplish but it is always an unpleasant and distasteful task. Do not, however, feel sorry for yourself or think of your feelings – the bird or animal feels worse.

Small birds are killed if the neck is pulled and twisted round.

Small animals – up to the size of a rat – can be held by the tail and swung sharply against a rock or hard surface.

Larger birds and animals must receive a sharp and heavy blow to the base of the skull with a rock, stone, stick or boot.

Do not be alarmed by the nerve reflex jerks and convulsions which always follow and last for a few seconds.

If an immediate and final solution is not required, then the first provision must be warmth and quiet. This is usually best provided by confinement in a box – the darkness gives security since nothing moving can be seen.

Most creatures seem to be soothed by the motion of being carried or transported.

Thus, treatment for 'shock' is usually the first requirement.

If limbs are broken, expert assistance will be required. If the fracture is high on a leg or wing then a bird will probably not recover enough to be released. This then presents a further problem which you must recognize and solve one way or the other.

Serious cuts or other injuries will probably result in the same situation.

Lesser injuries should be bathed in warm, slightly salted water, dried thoroughly and covered lightly if possible.

If the creature has no obvious injuries, then warmth and quiet are the first needs.

The problem is likely to be exposure (lack of food/warmth), disease or poisoning. Contamination of feathers or poisoning by oil is usually fatal. Most poisoning, which has enabled you to catch the creature, is also likely to result in death or permanent brain damage and consequent disability.

Disease usually has the same result and, if not, requires expert advice.

One common disease, which is easily recognized in birds, occurs most frequently in hot summer weather. This is coccidiosis – an infection of the alimentary tract which is debilitating and eventually fatal. It is highly infectious to other birds, and thus any bird that appears weak and has green-coloured droppings should be destroyed.

In extreme weather conditions weakness in animals and birds may result simply from lack of food, but at any other time may be due to disease.

Check the mouth and throat for any blockage, or the beak or teeth for deformity.

If the creature is too weak to eat by itself, or has lost any incentive to eat, it may be necessary to feed it forcibly. Hold the bill or mouth open and push small quantities of food well into the throat. It is sometimes better to ensure that the food is not cold, dipping it in warm water supplies moisture.

You may not be able to supply the natural food but at least ensure that you provide what is basically an equivalent food. Insect-eating birds are quite difficult to feed satisfactorily. There are proprietary brands of food for insect eaters which you can obtain from pet shops. Fine, raw mince or raw egg given with a dropper are makeshift alternatives. Beware of pouring water into a creature – wet food is always the best way of providing moisture. Tins of cat or dog foods are useful for many birds and animals. If a bird or animal is capable of feeding itself, it is wise to put the food down on the ground rather than on a nice clean plate. 'Dirt' from the ground will contain grit and mineral traces and also will be a more natural way of feeding for the animal. An extreme example is the case of some fox cubs who were fed 'good red meat' and began to develop rickets. What they needed was the more varied diet of road casualties – rabbits, squirrels and birds given whole. The intestines of the rabbit containing partly digested grass were usually the first to be eaten. Fruit and vegetables will also be acceptable. Most creatures have a far more varied diet than is generally supposed; for example, in September, fox droppings often contain a very high percentage of blackberry seeds.

The odd sick or injured creatures that we are concerned about are only a tiny fraction of the numbers that die naturally and, often, violently. Our attempts to save them are often an interference in the natural balance, since frequently they are the weaklings that predators would otherwise have eliminated.

Natural fluctuations of bird populations, usually resulting directly or indirectly from weather or climatic changes, are far more dramatic and devastating in their effect than the instinctive behaviour of your cat and account for thousands of deaths whereas your feline pet may only take a fraction of the number killed by indiscriminate use of pesticides in farming and market gardening.

When should we interfere?

Opposite page: The instinct to migrate is strong – the parents of this young fledgling swift departed for South Africa leaving it behind. Feeding such an insect eater is very difficult and it became gradually weaker and died – possibly it was a weakling!

Above: Most very young animals still taking milk can be fed and weaned on much the same foods as a human baby. Test whether milk needs to be richer or diluted. Calcium tablets may be necessary – crush them over the food.

Below: Leave young birds alone – their parents are always nearby. It is also unwise to feed them. Young birds, like this baby song thrush, are fed by their parents on animal protein.

Many birds that search the foliage of trees for food, breed in May when swarms of leaf caterpillars abound as food for their young. Insect eaters that feed on flying insects feed their young later, in June or July.

If food is scarce in May, because of bad weather, and the youngsters perish, there is still time for a second brood to be reared. Not so for the later breeding insect eaters; for them a week of cold weather can be disastrous.

But the fluctuations are usually self-balancing within a decade or two. A pair of chaffinches rearing a brood of five young is one unit of the total chaffinch population, most of whom are attempting to rear similarly sized families. Thus, the chaffinch population has the possibility of increasing by 250 per cent in thecourse of a few weeks.

However, the population never increases in this manner. By the following spring the population will be approximately the same as it was in the previous spring. Each family unit of seven must, on average, lose five of its members. This will happen through accidents (cars, wires, etc.), by predators, disease, food shortage or severe weather conditions.

In the long term the complicated balance is maintained. However, the vast changes in the environment that man is now capable of creating frequently upset this balance.

It is sometimes difficult to keep a clear perspective, especially when our reactions to suffering creatures are emotional.

A bird or animal is found

If a bird or animal allows us to approach it there is usually something seriously wrong with it unless it is a frightened youngster. Before picking it up you should ask yourself the following questions:

Is it a young one? Should I leave it where it is or put it in a safer place nearby?

Is it injured? Can I do anything for it or is it a hopeless case that should be put out of its misery?

If I take it home, can I do anything that will enable it to survive and recover enough to be released?

If not, am I prepared to look after it as long as it lives?

Flowering Plants

Flowering plants are divided into two broad groups, according to whether the first embryonic leaf (cotyledon) formed from the seed becomes one or a pair of leaves. Plants are thus called either monocotyledons (the seed is in one part) or dicotyledons (the seed splits into two parts).

Monocotyledons are usually narrow-leaved with parallel veins and the flower is in three parts. Monocotyledons include irises and many other water plants, lilies, daffodils, bluebells, tulips, orchids, rushes and grasses and cereal plants.

Dicotyledons form the larger group. Their leaves are net-veined and their flowers are in four or five parts. All trees are dicotyledons. Included in the group are daisies, roses, mints, buttercups, clovers, vetches, flowering shrubs and fruit bushes.

Many of the larger families have characteristic features.

Most of the flowers that have a four-petal shape, which produces a cross-like arrangement of the

flower, belong to the family *Cruciferae*. This is a large family which includes many common wild plants such as the cresses, the mustards, and the brassicas (cabbages). Many have a sharp taste; for instance, water cress, mustard and horseradish.

The daisy type of flower is easily recognized as a group – the *Compositae*. Many are popular garden flowers: asters, dahlias, sunflowers, marguerites and chrysanthemums. These plants have a composite flower head which is really a cluster of tube-like florets. The radiating shape of the flower attracts insects to its centre but a comparatively long 'tongue' is required to probe the tube of the floret for the flower's nectar, so only those insects with appropriate mouthparts visit the flower. On the other hand, a large group with very shallow flowers arranged on a many-branched, umbrella-spoked, flat head are visited by a host of flies, midges and small beetle. These are *Umbelliferae*, such as wild carrot, hedge parsley, fennel and caraway, including several herbs with strong related flavours used in cooking. Many of the family have a distinctive scent, and some have swollen starchy roots which have been developed as vegetables – carrot and parsnip, for example. However, the family also includes dangerous plants such as the poisonous hemlock.

The family *Rosaceae* includes, besides roses, most of the fruit-producing trees and shrubs, apple, cherry, pear, peach and plum. There are others, such as blackberry, raspberry and strawberry, as well as wild plants such as rowan, white beam, hawthorn, meadowsweet, the geums and cinquefoils.

An important family, well represented by cultivated plants, is the pea-flowered *Papilionaceae* which, besides the peas and all the various haricot, runner, broad and soya beans, also includes lentils and peanuts. Garden and wild flower representatives include lupins, brooms and gorse, and the vetches, lucernes, trefoils and clovers. The characteristic 'winged' butterfly-shaped flowers make this one of the easiest groups to recognize.

Two large families which are similar in several ways are the figworts and mints, forbiddingly named *Scrophulariaceae* and the *Labiatae*. The flowers are usually small, 'winged' and lipped around the entrance to a tube. Their stems are normally square.

Many of the mint family are strongly aromatic and include, besides the various mints, other herbs such as sage, thyme, basil, marjoram and balm. Among wild plants are the woundworts, germanders and the dead nettles (which are not closely related to stinging nettles).

Below: Fennel is a member of the easily recognized family, Umbelliferae, many of which are used as herbs in cooking. As the name suggests, the plants in this family have umbrella-shaped flower-heads. It is a tall plant and the leaves taste of aniseed.

The parts of a buttercup flower

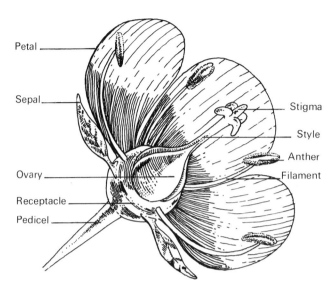

Petal
Sepal
Ovary
Receptacle
Pedicel
Stigma
Style
Anther
Filament

Right: The yellow flag which grows beside rivers and lakes is a monocotyledonous plant that has its flower parts in threes. The 'petals' that hang down as land-ing platforms for visiting insects are really sepals. The stigma and anther are arranged within the flower to make self pollination almost impossible.

Above: Most dicotyledonous plants, such as this wild dog-rose, have their flowers arranged in multiples of four or five. It is scented to attract insects which feed on the pollen, although the flower has no nectar.

Upper centre left: The lady's smock is related to the cress family, the Cruciferae, *all of which have four petals arranged in a cross formation.*

Upper centre right: The great stitchwort's star-like flowers are common in the hedgerows in early summer. It is a member of the 'pink' family; its five petals are each split.

Lower centre left: A garden variety of the aster family (Michaelmas daisy) which oc-curs wild in North America is a typical example of the Compositae, *where the centre of the flower is a mass of florets.*

Lower centre right: The cone flower, pictured here, is one of several species which once grew wild on the American prairie. It is another member of the Com-positae family. Related species are usually cultivated in gardens as rudbeckias.

Bottom left: The yellow dead-nettle, or yellow archangel, is a member of the large Labiatae family which all have square stems and very specialized flowers. The five petals are joined at the base to form a tube. The constricted throat of the tube gives the family its name, from the Greek word laimos. Two petals form the upper lobe or hood and three petals make up the lower lip.

Bottom right: The restharrow is a hairy, spiny member of the pea family that prefers a limy soil. The shape of the 'winged' flower is typical of the family.

Like animals, plants are specialized in many diverse ways; again, like animals, there are some that 'specialize' in being general, all-purpose plants that are successful in a wide range of conditions. There are plants that are modified to meet the particular environmental conditions in which they exist and there are plants that have developed certain adaptations and refinements of design which aid fertilization or wide distribution of the plant, giving it an advantage.

One of the most specialized groups of plants in meeting extreme environmental conditions is the cacti family – a group of over 1,500 species originating in the New World. Cacti are plants that can live for months or years without water in intense dry heat and cold and can then take immediate advantage of sudden rain to grow rapidly and bloom. Most cacti have adapted their swollen stems as water storage areas and their leaves have been reduced to protective spines; so, with no true leaves and the stem covered with a tough, waxy skin, they have little evaporation loss.

Some plants, which tend to grow in poor soils, might be deficient in minerals; by adapting themselves in various ways to 'capture' and digest the protein of insects they have overcome this problem. Both the sundews and the butterworts have developed sticky hairs on their leaves that trap insects as the leaf slowly curls inwards, while the pitcher plants are represented by one family in the Old World and another in the New World. In the case of

Top left: The hedge bindweed, or convolvulus, whose more tropical relatives include the morning glory and the sweet potato, is a great climber. A deeply rooted perennial, as every gardener knows, it climbs by twisting its shoot tightly in an anti-clockwise direction around any support it can find. Most bindweeds close at night or if there is a likelihood of rain, but the large white species illustrated here tends to stay open on bright moonlit nights and even in heavy rain. The flower has developed from five petals.

Centre left: The blackberry or bramble pictured here, like the loganberry, briars and other climbing plants, grows dual purpose thorns. These thorns are very efficient in holding the running sprays in position in the tangle of a hedgerow and are also a deterrent to browsing animals. Blackberries are a common sight in the hedgerows in late summer.

Centre right: Traveller's joy, a lover of lime soils, is a wild clematis which climbs by twisting its leaf stalks around any available support. The feathery seeds give rise to another of its popular names – 'old man's beard'. 'Devil's hair' refers to the poisonous content of all parts of the plant which can be purgative, blistering, ulcerating and even fatal. Similar species can be found in North America as well as Britain.

Bottom left: White bryony is not related to its namesake, but is a member of the gourd family and its method of climbing is by tendrils which change their direction of twist halfway along their length. Like black bryony it has separate male and female flowers and its root and red berries are also poisonous. It is commonly said that fifteen berries are always a fatal dose for a child, and forty for an adult. Thus it is well named the 'devil's turnip'.

the pitcher plants the trap is formed from leaves adapted into slippery, water-filled tubes in which the insect drowns and is digested.

Many of the pitcher plants are epiphytic; that is, they grow on the branches of trees, as do many ferns and tropical orchids. This is an adaptation to the environment of the tropical forest. On the branches of trees there is more light and a greater chance of pollination by insects.

In temperate woods and hedgerows, there are many plants that elevate themselves by climbing on other plants.

Most commonly noticed are brambles and briars, whose thorns are not only protective but also the means by which blackberries and wild roses are able to climb to decorate bushes and hedges. Roots are adapted in plants, such as the ivy, to enable them to climb. Contrary to popular belief, the ivy is not a parasite in the sense that it 'feeds' off its supporting tree. It has its tree roots in the ground and those produced along the stem are merely used as anchors for climbing. Similarly the virginia creeper has its roots in the soil but has developed sucker pads to facilitate climbing.

Several climbing plants simply twist their growing shoot around a support. The best known examples are probably the runner bean and the less desirable convolvulus, both of which twist in an anti-clockwise direction. However, the honeysuckle and the hop entwine themselves in a clockwise direction.

Tendrils are a most ingenious form of suspension climbing. The pea has adapted its leaves into tendrils; other plants have formed them from leaf stalks or the stem.

Among the cultivated plants which have developed coiled tendrils for climbing are the marrow, cucumber and gourds. In the woods and fields, the related white bryony, which has male and female flowers on separate plants, climbs similarly by tendrils which begin by turning one way and then change and turn in the other direction. Black bryony, which is not the same family – being related to the yams – does not climb by tendrils but twists its shoot in a clockwise direction around a support.

Adaptation to conditions is well developed in aquatic and waterside plants. The majority of plants that grow beside the water are tall, stiff and erect, and thus unlikely to be affected by the lapping movement of the water or by changes in its level. Aquatic plants, growing deeper in the water, will have waxy leaves that float, such as the water lilies, or, if submerged, will be either flexible, rubbery and strap-like, or finely divided and feathery – both are forms of growth that will offer little resistance to the flow or movement of water. Some water plants change their leaf shape according to whether it is above or below the surface. The water crowfoot, a member of the buttercup family, *Ranunculaceae*, is a good example of such adaptation. Many submerged aquatic plants will push their flower head well clear of the water surface to increase the chances of pollination by either wind or insects. Nature is geared for survival, and plant life, like animal life, takes maximum advantage of the available environmental conditions.

The purpose of a flower head on a plant is to achieve the pollination of the embryonic seeds and the provision of a protective container during their growth. Plants are highly specialized to meet both these aims and the final dispersal of the seed.

Pollination is usually either by wind or insects. Those plants that have separate male and female flowers and depend on the wind have little need of a large, petalled female flower. All that is required is a prominent stigma to catch the pollen, and also large quantities of pollen. The male or pollen-bearing flower is usually large and accessible to the wind. Many trees and grasses are in this category; these are the pollen producers responsible for hay fever.

Plants that are dependent on insects for pollination often have large, colourful or conspicuous flowers to attract the insects. To aid in this they have a scent and a supply of nectar. These plants are dependent upon a particular insect – that is, deep probing nectar seekers or insects who are also attracted to carrion and, to us, even less pleasant fare – and have adapted their scents to be either sweet and fragrant or less 'pleasant' to attract the carrion feeders. Nectar, a sugary liquid easily converted into honey, is produced by flowers to entice insects to visit them in order 'accidentally' or incidentally to transfer pollen from the male flower, or male part of the flower where both parts are in one flower, to the female flower or part. For the flower, it is important that the nectar is supplied only to those insects for whom the pollen-bearing parts are specifically adapted. For instance, if the stamens of a flower were designed to daub pollen on large insects, the nectar would be quickly used up if smaller creatures could gain free access to it without touching the stamens. Thus many flowers have various arrangements and devices to 'select' the right insect to reach the nectar and to restrict others.

This specialization reaches its highest point in the complex adaptations of the orchids. These

Colourful and strikingly marked flowers have one purpose – to pollinate the ova that will become seeds. Colour and pattern are used to attract insects and to point the way to the flower's nectar store, which is bait to secure fertilization. Insects' sight is different from ours. We believe that none but butterflies can see red; many insects, and certainly bees, can see ultra-violet light which is invisible to us. Red flowers appear to be black to bees and other insects, and white flowers, greenish. Many flowers, which to us are almost the same colour throughout, appear strikingly patterned to these insects because some parts reflect more ultra-violet light than others. This is especially true of violet and blue flowers. The pattern radiates from the honey source – the nectar, – and guides the visiting insect to obtain it; cross fertilization occurs incidentally during this process. The photographs of flowers show various patterns and structural arrangements to aid pollination by the 'right' insects. Reading from top, left to right: Oriental poppy, hollyhock, honeysuckle, flag iris, sea bindweed, bog bean, passion flower flowers have so developed that many of them need to be pollinated by one particular species of insect. Often, only this species will make the perfect fit to enter the orchid and receive the pollen on exactly the right spot to touch the stigma (tip of the female part) of the next orchid it visits. Many orchids have developed a resemblance to their particular insect, so as to attract it by deception.

The simplest method by which the flower avoids self-pollination and secures cross-pollination by another flower (prevention of 'in-breeding') is by a difference in timing between the production of pollen and the 'ripeness' of the female part for fertilization. Usually the pollen is only discharged after the ovary of seeds has been fertilized with pollen from another flower. One of the most involved methods of providing cross-pollination is that adopted by the cuckoopint, which virtually traps flies that have fertilized it, and then re-anoints them with its own pollen.

All the markings on a flower, its shape and even 'mechanism' (as in the antirrhinum) are beautifully suited to the purpose of attracting insects. Careful watching of the insects and a close examination of the flower will provide fascinating discoveries. There is nothing haphazard in the markings, colouration and format of a flower. All its aspects are a response to natural conditions and are designed to give the plant its best possible chances of survival and reproduction.

Above: The purplish spike (spadix) in the centre of the cuckoopint flower gives off a carrion-like smell which attracts flies into the cowl-shaped spathe. They pass through the neck into the bulbous lower section.

Below: If the cuckoo-pint is cut open, a strange structure can be seen. The fly pushes past the hair-like protuberances, which give to allow entry but deter exit. The fly, seeking the nectar from the bottom of its prison, leaves the pollen that it carried in on its legs and body from a previous visit to another flower on the ripe stigmas (left hand specimen). When fertilization is finished, the anthers – the purple area in the middle – burst forth with pollen and re-dust the flies (centre). Later, the hair-like structures at the entrance wither and allow the fly to escape (right) to enter and pollinate another flower. This partnership ensures cross-pollination between flowers; for the fly, it ensures security from enemies, nectar for food and, maybe, companionship.

Methods of seed dispersal are just as diverse as methods of pollination. Many tree seeds are winged but most of the small plants that depend on the wind have a feathery 'parachute'-borne seed. Others use an 'explosive' flick, whereby a pod type of seed-box increases tensions in the pod case as it dries, and then breaks apart suddenly, shooting out the seed. In order to observe this, watch gorse pods on a hot sunny day.

Various forms of hooks and barbs have been developed to catch in the fur of passing animals. Anyone who owns a dog knows that! But in most cases a magnifying lens is required to see the barbs – they are so tiny.

Usually, seeds that are buried in the pulp of a fruit have a tough indigestible covering. When a bud or animal eats the fruit, it also swallows the seed inside. Because the outer coat of the seed resists the digestive juices, the seed passes through the animal's body and is deposited far from the parent plant. After a fierce forest fire has burnt and destroyed all plant life in an area, often the first new, colonizing plants reappear around burnt stumps on which birds have perched!

Above left: The dandelion's globe-shaped head of down is well known, but is worthy of close examination. Each seed has a delicately feathered 'parachute' to carry it far and wide. The seed itself is pointed and barbed so that, once it has landed, it can only move deeper into the soil.

Top: The thistle family also produce heads of feathered seeds which are carried by the wind, as every farmer knows. Thistles which are cut down too early send up several new heads to replace the original one, but 'cut in July – they are sure to die'.

Above: Rose-bay willowherb or 'fire-weed' has a seed pod that splits open when dry and allows a host of feathered seeds to escape. The light, wind-borne seed can travel great distances.

Mistletoe, which is a parasitic plant that grows into the host tree, taking nutriment from it, has very sticky seeds in its fruit. Birds, such as the mistle-thrush, so named because of its liking for mistletoe berries, spread the seeds to other trees. As they try to clean their beaks on the branches they deposit the sticky seeds in suitable cracks – just where the mistletoe needs to grow!

Most nuts, such as the walnut and almond, have a surrounding case. Like the fleshy pulp of a plum, this serves as a covering for the kernel (the seed).

Top right: Himalayan or Indian balsam, like other balsams, has explosive seeds which burst at the touch of a hand, scattering the seed. If removed very carefully, they burst after a moment of warmth from the hand – hence the name, 'Jumping Jack'. On hot days in summer the twisting tensions in the drying seed pods cause them to crack open with a sudden 'explosive' force.

Centre left: The burs of burdock are well known to every boy as a missile and to every girl as something which is difficult to remove from her hair. The hooks are so sharp that they seem to stick to the skin.

Centre right: Clusters of the poisonous red berries of cuckoo-pint are a familiar sight in August hedgerows. These are poisonous to humans and many animals, and are left untouched by most birds.

Bottom: The long sharp spikes of the gorse or furze, which is a member of the pea family, are a thoroughly effective protection against grazing animals.

However, as nuts are usually not swallowed whole or are taken away, their case may be eaten, and thus the covering does not have the same function. Many nuts are destroyed as seeds by being eaten. Presumably, in the process sufficient numbers survive by being dropped, buried or stored, away from the parent plant, to make the provision of nuts a worthwhile process that ensures the plant's survival as a species.

Most seeds are transported away from the plants that grew them by animals or birds or by the wind. One of the strangest methods of using the wind is that of the North American tumbleweed, which is detached at the roots and then blown about by the wind, scattering its seeds as it goes.

Very few plants use water as a major means of distributing seed. However quite a lot of plants use it almost accidentally, as may be seen by following a stream. Plants may be found growing on or near the banks of a stream, which are alien to the surrounding landscape. The seeds are carried in the water itself by the stream and the plants soon become widespread along its banks.

Seeds must have certain protective qualities. A very tough skin is an almost universal requirement, while the seed itself is usually very hard with a low water content. Protection is thus obtained against accidental damage by wind or other cause of movement; extremes of temperature; drought; and fungus. Seeds are also usually capable of remaining dormant until conditions are right for germination – even over many years, in some cases.

Plants themselves have evolved various protective devices. The most common are thorns, spines and barbs. Many cacti have numerous fine needles that are brittle and may even be barbed at the ends. The stinging nettle has fine needle-like stinging glands, the ends of which break off and inject the acid that causes familiar blistering of the skin.

'Poison ivy' and 'poison oak', which are American shrubs of the sumac family, produce a highly irritating oil which can have a far worse effect than stinging nettles after only slight contact. Many plants have a covering of fine hairs on the stems and leaves to discourage small creatures from climbing up to take pollen or nectar. Often, for the same purpose, flowers themselves are protected by a hairy surface, especially at the entrance to the flower.

So many plants manufacture poisonous substances that these substances must have a protective function that is advantageous to the plant. Some animals and birds are affected by the poisons, some are not. The seeds and needles of the yew are poisonous to cattle but birds that eat the red berries are unaffected: unlike the fruit, the seeds are not digested and they pass through the bird.

Life within the Wood

Trees are not only the largest form of life on this planet, but they also live the longest. The largest and oldest are two species of sequoias growing on the west coast of the United States of America. Some coastal redwoods grow to 100 metres (300 feet) high and may be over 2,000 years old. The tallest, which measures 112 metres (364 feet) high, is a mere youngster of 500 years. Another species of sequoia, the wellingtonia of the Sierra Nevada in California, is even older – estimates vary between 3,500 and possibly 4,000 years old. Even prime oak trees of a mere 150 years, the right age to be used for timber, are old enough to be felled by the great, great grandchildren of the men who planted them!

Although trees have an obvious economic value, with 85 per cent of the population of Britain living in urban areas which cover 15 per cent of the land surface, they also have an amenity value. This becomes more significant when we consider that there is only one acre of woodland for every 30 people of the population; in Germany there is one acre for every eight people and in the United States there are four acres of forest for each person.

Five thousand years ago, before man became a Neolithic farmer who cleared the ground to grow crops, much of Europe was covered with forests. Britain was mostly oak woodland, although previously other species such as birch, pine, hazel and lime had been among the dominant species.

It would have been possible in Britain, Europe and the United States for a squirrel to have travelled hundreds, or even thousands, of miles without touching the ground, merely jumping from branch to branch.

Today, the remaining woodland consists of islands of trees in an ocean of fields dominated by a few crop plants, just as urban parks are open spaces, among buildings with islands of trees. This is how our wildlife must see the countryside – dotted with pockets of safety.

Far left: This giant sequoia or wellingtonia, called 'General Sherman', is over 3,500 years old. It is 83 m (252 ft) high and 24 m (79 ft) in girth. It is the oldest and biggest (in bulk) living thing in the world. The wellingtonias grow in the deep, wide canyons of the Sierra Nevada in North America. The tallest trees in the world, Sequoia sempervirens or the coastal redwoods, also grow in California. These trees flourish in the narrow strip of land between the Pacific Ocean and the coastal mountains, which receives 250 cm (100 in) of rain annually.

Above left: Many large areas of hill country are being replanted with trees. Conifers are often chosen because they are quicker growing and thus more profitable. The largest man-made forest (replanted) in Europe is the Keilder Forest in Northumberland, which runs along the border between England and Scotland. In Britain, the Forestry Commission has replanted acres of woodland.

Below left: Most of the ancient upland forests of oak and ash were cleared centuries ago to provide valuable sheep grazing – now only small relic woods remain. During the Middle Ages vast flocks of sheep and a larger human population lived in such rural areas.

Above: Large stretches of woodland still exist in the countryside but little or none of it is completely natural. Although most of it has been planted for timber, or to provide shelterbelts, small patches have survived as fox coverts in hunting country or shooting preserves for rearing pheasants. A large proportion is scrub that grows where the land is not worth cultivating, and a lot of the countryside's 'woodland' is in linear form as hedges. All such land, however, provides a refuge for varied wildlife and much of it has an important and valuable amenity and leisure function for society, especially in areas containing public footpaths and bridleways.

Right: Most large modern cities contain some wild life that survives only because it is versatile and adaptable. This is demonstrated by such creatures as house sparrows, starlings, pigeons, mice, rats, cockroaches and house flies which have survived successfully to the point of becoming pests that no longer qualify for the term 'wild life' in the usual sense. Sometimes it is difficult to imagine how any animals can survive in such man-made deserts of concrete and glass cliffs with little or no green vegetation. The photograph on the right shows an aerial view of part of Chicago.

A wood is more than a given number of trees growing near each other – like a pond or an island, it is a world in itself. Some things enter and leave it but many do not. Of course, some external influences are exerted upon it, such as the sun, the rain and the wind.

The trees themselves are affected differently. The tree on the edge of the wood may not grow in the same way, or be the same shape, as a tree in the centre of the wood. The trees on the northern edge are different from those on the southern perimeter.

Thus there are many variations in a single wood.

Young trees growing near slightly older, and therefore taller trees, will not have the same chance as young trees growing near an old and dying tree which will soon leave a gap through which light will come.

Thus, although each individual tree is different and interacts with its neighbours, it is still part of a larger unit – the wood – which, in turn, has its own characteristics and also influences within itself which are constantly creating changes.

Above: Ancient open deciduous woodland of oak and pollarded hornbeam trees. With natural re-generation, there are age variations and more than one layer of vegetation.

Below: This photograph shows naturally regenerating wood-land after old trees have been removed to increase light young birch and holly are grow-ing under oak and hornbeam.

Top: This area of ancient beech woodland has suffered in autumn gales, but the light can reach the forest floor so that warm sunlight can germinate young seedling trees and start the forest growth cycle once again. Such cycles vary according to the type of woodland but, in this case, where the beech is the climax species, it may be at least two hundred years between the recolonization of bare ground by the first species and the fall of the mature beech trees.

Above: Some trees, like the beech, allow very little light to penetrate and thus mosses are usually the only plants that can grow in beech woodlands. But when a mature tree is killed by fungus infection or is uprooted by strong winds a gap is left in the canopy, and in the resulting patch of sunlight grow numerous plants such as grasses, rushes, brambles, the willow herb, young birches and willows. Thus the forest growth cycle has already started again.

Right: Only on the edges of coniferous woodland is there enough light for ground vegetation to grow. Closely growing trees may compete for the light in the depths of the woods where little light can penetrate – while the side branches die, only the top is green and stretches straight up towards the sunlight. These are the conditions required for the quick growth of straight, clean timber in woodlands and forest.

An area of coniferous woodland is clearly very different from deciduous woodland, through which the light can penetrate fully for at least six months of the year. There are also great differences in the deciduous wood according to which species is dominant. Beech allows very little summer light to filter through to the forest floor and, while oak trees permit lighter conditions, birch woodland has even more light and hence further variations in the ground vegetation.

The topsoil itself may vary with different tree species; for instance, beech trees produce a leaf mould that tends to be more acid than other trees. In woods where the trees are all of a similar age, the conditions and hence the undergrowth will tend to be uniform throughout the woodland. In woodland with the same dominant species of tree, but with a wide age range, the undergrowth will be more varied.

Some woodland will have a cover of ground vegetation, perhaps grass or wild garlic or only bluebells as a spring and early summer carpet. Other woodland may have an undergrowth of bramble or bracken or honeysuckle; a shrub layer of holly or hazel may be present; or an under canopy of one tree species may struggle and survive beneath a higher canopy of another species.

Above: Mature beech woodland with a closed canopy and no ground layer or undergrowth because of the lack of light. Only moss will be able to grow in these conditions.

Upper left: In this woodland, with a high closed canopy of oak and ash trees which are among the last trees to break into leaf, the sun can reach the ground layer of plants until late in the spring. This allows wild garlic, wood anemones and celandine to form a carpet of flowers.

Below left: While fallen timbers lie rotting, a thick carpet of beech seedlings will grow on, forming an undergrowth from which only a handful will survive and, through natural selection of the most vigorous, become mature trees. The photograph shows a good germination year – weather conditions cause great variations from year to year.

Below right: Young beech seedlings pushing through the carpet of last year's leaves. Several still have 'hoods' of the seed case which the first leaves have yet to dislodge.

Above, below left, below right: Wood sorrel, wood anemone and wild garlic are spring flowers that frequently grace woodlands. Wood sorrel, being sensitive to rain and darkness, contracts in these conditions; the wood anemone turns away from the wind. Their delicate charm equals that of exotic blooms.

Different layers of vegetation may exist together, and it will be found that each layer has its own population of insects and even birds. The high canopy of the dominant trees will be the feeding ground of some of the tit family, the blue, longtailed and coal tits. During the caterpillar period in the summer, there will be an influx of starlings, sparrows and finches to join the leaf warblers – the chiffchaffs, willow and wood warblers – feeding on the insect population of the upper layer of the wood.

The great tit and marsh tit tend to feed more in the middle, shrub layer and on the ground. Also feeding in the shrub layer will be thrushes, blackbirds, robins and dunnocks. At this level, below the canopy, the flycatchers will hawk for insects; the redstarts, nightingales and warblers, such as the blackcap and garden warbler, will also frequent the middle layer. Woodpeckers, nuthatches and tree creepers will work over the trunks and branches in search of food.

Down on the ground and in the field or herb layer, other birds will feed, varying from the wren to the woodpigeon. But there will be some overlapping, according to the season, by greenfinches and chaffinches, great tits and marsh tits, thrushes, blackbirds and robins. The ground is a richer hunting ground in the autumn and winter, when fruits and seeds and over-wintering insects can all be found in the leaf-litter.

Conditions in a wood can change radically in the space of a decade. Managed woodland, changed by man, will be quite different from an old and long established woodland area where natural change has gradually created very varied conditions.

Even the ground beneath one tree can vary significantly and produce more ground vegetation under its southern branches than in the shade of those on the northern side. Because of this, the chemical value of the soil on one side of the tree may differ from that on the other. Of course, there are also obvious differences between coniferous and deciduous woodlands. Wild life and plant life vary and, indeed, quite different patterns of life and vegetation can occur in an individual woodland.

Left, reading from top to bottom: In ten years, these young birch trees growing in the clearing have formed a dense thicket. The top photograph was taken in 1964, the second five years later and the third in 1974. The clearing had existed for many years – rabbits, deer and browsing cattle maintaining a balance except where bramble slowly encroached on the grass. A fire burnt the bramble and heather, the rabbits were decimated by disease, the deer disappeared and the bare burnt soil was quickly colonized by birch seed. In these circumstances birch is frequently the first tree to appear as its fine wind-borne seed can travel considerable distances. Only the strongest birches in the thicket will grow tall to full maturity. Birch, with its distinctive white bark, is an extremely fast growing tree.

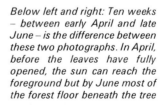

Above from left to right. The changes in woodland that accompany the seasonal pattern are startling when we are reminded of them by photographs taken in January (top left), June (top right), September (above left) and November (above right). This old hornbeam woodland allows enough light to penetrate to the moist forest floor for grasses to grow. The trees are pollards: lopping the branches back every 15–20 years was an ancient custom. It was last done 100 years ago.

Below left and right: Ten weeks – between early April and late June – is the difference between these two photographs. In April, before the leaves have fully opened, the sun can reach the foreground but by June most of the forest floor beneath the tree is in deep shadow. It is no coincidence that most woodland flowers bloom early when they can still receive the spring sunshine before the thick leaf canopy forms. This is just part of the inter-related pattern of woodland life.

Wild life The wood plays a very definite rôle in relation to the land around it. In many respects it is a refuge for wildlife – for some to rest in the daytime, for others to sleep at night. For many it may be a secure fortress from which to sally forth to raid the surrounding fields. For smaller, sedentary creatures it may constitute their entire world, which they will never leave.

The population of small mammals in an area of woodland is an important ecological factor. They are almost certain to be present in the ground vegetation of any woodland, and are more numerous than might be assumed by a casual inspection. Although voles are about in daytime, the wood mouse is more nocturnal. A rustling in the leaf litter on the forest floor that suddenly stops will soon resume if one is completely still and quiet – then, close observation is often possible. The field vole, bank vole and wood mouse populations consume great amounts of seeds, nuts and fruits and, in hard weather, roots, bark and shoots; insects form an important part of their diet in summer. They are truly omnivorous in their diets.

In this way, these small mammals contribute to the balance of life in the woods. They are not a threat to that balance but are part of it, as they have evolved within the woodland communities for thousands of years. Because they can increase their numbers quickly, they undoubtedly help to iron out some of the fluctuations of plant, tree and insect growth and reproduction, caused by the weather and other factors. We know little of how important they are: certainly we do not know much about the quantity of insects consumed, but in captivity they will eat a considerable amount of animal protein. However, they are also important in the rôle they play as prey for many of the predators. This is especially true since myxomatosis drastically reduced the rabbit population. They are a major food source for many birds and mammals who include foxes, stoats, weasels, hawks and owls and are attacked by many other animals, including crows, herons, hedgehogs, badgers and snakes.

Above: The dormouse, rare and also very local in distribution, with a warm brown colouring, has a distinctive furry tail. Dormice hibernate from October until the warm, sunny days of the following spring. During this period of deep sleep their body temperature falls to match their surroundings. They seem to prefer woodland with hazel and undergrowth of honeysuckle.

Left: The other group of small mammals that are common everywhere are the shrews, but they are not closely related to mice or voles. They are easily recognizable by their velvet-like coats, long pointed snouts and minute eyes. Feeding in tunnels below the leaves, on all kinds of invertebrates but particularly worms, they are extremely active and hunt night and day for food with short rest periods of twenty minutes or so every hour. In the space of twenty-four hours they will consume their own weight in food.

Top (left and right): Voles can be distinguished from mice by their comparatively short tails, blunt furry faces and lack of prominent ears. The bank vole (left) has a more chestnut brown colouring than the field vole (right) and tends to be noticeably whiter underneath. The most accurate clue to identifying the species is the tail. In the field vole it is only one third the length of the body, while the bank vole's tail is half as long as its body and also has white hairs underneath, black on top and a wispy tuft of black hairs at the tip. The field vole feeds largely on grass and grass roots and lives in fields and rough grassland. The bank vole lives in hedgerows and open woodland preferring fruits and seeds to grass.

Above (left and right): A mouse is a small mammal with a long tail and prominent ears such as a wood mouse (left) or a common house mouse (right). The main

difference between these two is the large eyes of the wood mouse. It also has chestnut-brown fur rather than the grey-brown of the house mouse. The white underparts and feet of the wood mouse are further confirmation of its identity. Sometimes, especially in the autumn, wood mice will tend to enter outhouses, sheds and even houses. They will not establish themselves or cause a great deal of damage. The greyer house mouse has a 'meaner' look and unpleasant smell, and it causes more damage and even danger from contamination of food. '

Below: The harvest mouse is extremely small and rather ginger-coloured. It often uses its tail when moving about in vegetation. However, it is very local and is not often found in woodland, preferring tall, rough grassland, reedbeds and cornfields. Harvest mice build a round ball-like nest of grass.

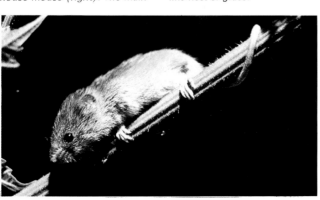

Watching animals at night

Make your first attempt in summer – between May and September. First visit the spot in daylight, a few days before you intend to watch. If you wish to take a companion, choose one who is as keen as you are and who knows how to keep quiet.' If you know where there is an active badger sett, an occupied fox earth, or a favourite clearing in which deer feed, then you have a slight advantage. However, there is no need to worry if you do not know of such a place. Choose the edge of a wood, sit against a large tree on the western side (anywhere between south-west and north, as the sun sets in the north-west in summer and the sky continues to give light after darkness has fallen). Pick a position where you have clear views in several directions. If necessary, remove a little vegetation that might obstruct your view – not too much, though. Decide how you are going to approach your position quietly and without crossing an area you may wish to watch, as your footsteps will leave a scent.

You must wait patiently for a still, calm and warm night. If there is the slightest breeze, then your approach may have to be re-thought so that you walk *into* the breeze. You should then watch in the direction from which the wind is coming. Set off in time to reach your watching station at least half an hour before sunset. Sit near your companion so that you can signal by a slight touch – without sound or movement. If you *must* move, choose a moment when the animal is looking away – remember that some animals (deer and hares) can see 'sideways' without pointing their faces at you. When you do move, make sure it is 'painfully' slowly and thus unnoticed.

Now all you need to do is wait. Relax, listen to the last song birds, see others flying to their roosts, watch the subtle changes of colour in the sky and landscape, hear the distant noises of man, and *then* gradually become aware of small noises around you. Keep your eyes open now, as creatures may appear in front of you without any warning or sound. Good watching!

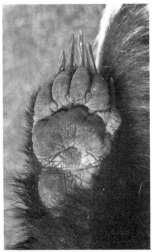

Above: The badger is the largest predator in Britain and, apart from rare animals like the lynx, wolf and brown bear, the largest common carnivore in Europe. It is largely nocturnal, spending the day deep in its complex tunnels and chambers, which can sometimes be centuries old. The badger does little harm and often a great deal of good. Its diet consists mainly of earthworms, young rabbits, rats, mice, voles, hedgehogs, frogs, slugs, snails, wasp grubs and beetles, and also vegetable material such as fruit, acorns and bluebell bulbs. Thus the badger is really omnivorous (eating both animal and plant foods) in its eating habits and diet.

Far left: The photograph shows the forefoot of a badger, showing the long claws used for digging and the broad pad with five toes which give the badger's footprint its distinctive shape.

Near left: A well-used badger sett will have easily identifiable signs showing which entrances are regularly used. Place a twig across the holes a few nights before watching and return the following day. The twigs that are moved will point to the best hole to observe. This photograph is taken immediately above an entrance and shows the numerous footprints of the badger left by the creatures going in and out of the sett.

Large carnivores have long disappeared from Britain, most of Europe and all but the remote parts of North America. Very few are present in sufficient numbers to have a significant effect on the woods or countryside today. One of the smallest carnivores is the weasel which gives its name to a group of predatory animals which include the wolverine, the badger, the martens, the polecat, minks and stoats. Most have disappeared and exist only in remote places – the pine marten and polecat still survive in mountainous areas of Britain in small numbers, but they are more common in Europe. In past centuries they have been persecuted by man wherever the woods are preserved for game. Stoats and weasels, however, perhaps because they are smaller and can hide more easily, have been more successful. They

seem to appear and disappear in an area according to the fluctuations of the rabbit and mole populations. Myxomatosis may also have affected the stoat, as rabbits accounted for a large part of its food. Unless you know the whereabouts of a lair, these animals are difficult to find and watch.

Foxes, too, have been affected by the loss of rabbits but they have adapted to this change and seem to be no less numerous. They – and the omnivorous badger – will have their earths and setts within a wood and between dusk and dawn may range across the countryside in search of food. But even they will have their regular territories and these territorial 'single zones' will be systematically covered and marked in the fox's nightly hunt for his food across open fields and woodland.

Above: A polecat ferret. Bred originally from the wild polecat, ferrets have been used by man for centuries to flush rabbits from their burrows into nets. Albino ferrets have been favoured in selected breeding. Feral ferrets, that have 'gone wild', are surprisingly common. The wild polecat occurs throughout Europe but in Britain is now confined to mid-Wales and the Welsh border. It belongs to the family that includes the weasel, otter and badger, and, in north Scandinavia, the wolverine and, in North America, the skunk. Like the skunk, the polecat has a powerful anal scent gland which is used to mark territory.

What you need to watch animals at night

If you wish to see some of the more shy creatures of a wood, you require the following equipment:

Cushion – plus patience; your body will need the cushion not only for comfort but also to prevent fidgeting as you will need to remain perfectly still for long periods of time.

Clothing – more than you expect, as sitting still becomes a chilly occupation even on summer nights and to cover as much of you as possible from insect attack.

Insect repellant – for your face and ears, which you cannot cover as you need all your senses to be alert and sharp.

Binoculars – if you can take binoculars they will be especially useful if they 'increase' the amount of light available by concentrating it. Most modern binoculars do this. See page 35.

Torch – needed only for an emergency. Do not use it unless you really must. It will destroy your night vision and it will be 15 or 20 minutes before you can see as clearly in the dark again. Red paper or plastic tied over your torch will not alarm the animals as much as white light.

Notebook and pencil – so that, when you finish watching and before you go home, you can write down all you have seen while it is fresh in your memory.

Although all these creatures influence the overall pattern of life in the wood, each in their own particular, albeit indirect, way, there are some that affect the woodland itself in a very direct way. Hares, rabbits and deer, by their browsing and grazing – also part of the pattern – continue to affect growth and regeneration of young trees, just as did the grazing cattle of the early farmers who first began clearing the woodlands, which they usually referred to as 'the waste'. In fact, the steady grazing by the cattle was often the gradual clearing process, the final felling of the trees was merely the end. Deer, rabbits and hares tend to have a similar effect, if their numbers are great enough, by affecting the undergrowth and young trees and at least changing the character of a woodland, although not clearing it as did the cattle.

Deer, which may now be present in greater numbers over a wider area than they have been for many centuries, use woodland as a daytime refuge, grazing and browsing out in the more open country-side between sunset and sunrise. However, they, too, are creatures of habit, feeding and resting in an area which suits them and which they know very well. Only when there is a severe change, disturb-ance or interruption in their lives are they found wandering widely into unexpected areas.

Woodland, then, is a very variable factor in the landscape, with a changing internal pattern of life. In some ways the creatures – animals and birds and insects – that it shelters have an effect on the surrounding countryside. In another respect, how-ever, the wood is an isolated oasis, a relic of the natural communities of plants and animals that were once more widespread over the British landscape.

Top left: The brown hare, often thought of as an animal of an open agricultural landscape, frequently inhabits woodland. It sometimes feeds there – especially in bad weather – and often it lies up in woods be-tween feeds. Bark, bramble, stems and even young holly growth are part of their winter feed, plus other selected plants.

Top: Once familiar, the rabbit is now seen less often. Although the hare is larger, this difference in identification is not always obvious. A safer distinction is the warmer brown of the hare's fur and the longer hindlegs and ears of the hare.

Opposite: In the man-occupied countryside of lowland areas, deer lie up in woods during the day. When disturbed they usu-ally run into the centre of a field to obtain the maximum warning of the approach of danger. This photograph of a wild fallow deer was taken only 25 km (16 miles) from the centre of London.

Above: These are particularly clear tracks of a fallow deer in the sand beside a stream. The tracks, or 'slots', of deer are the usual indications of their being in an area. Sharp eyes will often detect deer droppings, which are confirmation of this presence.

A page from a night-watcher's notebook

(A typical June evening in southern England) Weather: warm, still and sunny.

Half the field and distant hillside are still covered with sunshine. Rustling leaves in nearby brambles – probably a bank vole.

Many birds are still singing. Wood pigeons are flying in to roost in the wood behind.

A brown hare moves slowly across the field in front. A robin and a thrush are still singing. The sun has set – colours are fading.

Something is moving through the wood behind – twigs are crackling quite loudly – probably deer.

Another hare runs across the field.

A tawny owl is calling in the wood. Another calls further away. A nightingale is singing in the distance. Still light, although all the daylight has gone.

There seems to be a pale patch in the entrance to the badger's sett – badger's face perhaps?

There are sudden thudding noises – one hare, then another, rushes past – three metres away – down the bank and into the wood. Perhaps a territorial chase? There are no signs of danger!

It is just possible to see the silhouette of a fallow deer against the sky along the edge of the wood. Now there are two more. They are moving out into the field feeding as they go.

The badger is out! The head has come out, it sniffed around several times and disappeared. One badger has now come straight out, stood giving a good view before trundling down the path to the left. It squatted down twice to mark the path with scent.

Another large badger has come out – he went quickly over the bank and disappeared.

Several deer – at least eight – are in the field – one buck is grazing quite near.

A large owl has just flown along the edge of the wood – probably a tawny owl.

There is a sudden crashing in the wood just behind – now the sharp alarm bark of fallow deer.

A gentle breeze is now blowing from the field – the fallow deer in the wood must have caught my scent. The deer have now vanished from the field, too. It is unlikely that the badgers will appear again until almost dawn. Time to go home now. It has been a good night's watching.

Life within a Tree

The tree as a community During May, it is sometimes necessary, when walking through an oak wood, to brush aside a curtain of silk threads, each of which is held taut by the swinging body of a green caterpillar. On a still day, it is often possible to hear the hiss and crackle of thousands of defoliating caterpillars chewing away in the leaf canopy above and their frass, or droppings, pattering down to the woodland floor. The oak roller moth is one of several species from whose eggs hatch the swarms of caterpillars that festoon the trees during some springs. One biologist has calculated that one moth may lay as many as 2,000 eggs. This must mean that, on average, the caterpillar's chances of survival to an adult moth are 1,998 to 2 – as the species only require the survival of two to replace the male and female who were responsible for the eggs!

But it is only when favourable conditions produce exceptional numbers of caterpillars, and the trees are almost stripped of leaves, that we notice what is happening above our heads. Then we realize that not only is there a community of life in a woodland, but there is also a community living in each tree. In fact, it is more correct to say that there are several communities in a tree.

When we consider the varying needs of the host of creatures living in and on and under a tree, it becomes clear that, from the point of view of a small insect, one place in the tree is very different from another. The larvae that live under the bark in darkness and a relatively even temperature exist in different conditions from those that the purple hairstreak butterfly enjoys as it flits in the sunshine around the top of the oak tree, feeding on the 'honey dew' secretions of the aphids that, in turn, feed on the juices of the leaves and shoots. Honey dew is the sweet sticky coating that often covers leaves (and parked cars) in summer.

Those are the extreme differences. There are more subtle ones: the top of the leaf is in the sun with slightly more movement of air across it than the shady and rather more humid conditions on the surface of the underside of the leaf – crucial differences for a minute insect larva. Generally, one can identify five main areas – what the biologist calls 'micro-habitats' – about a tree which are very different places in which to live. These are the foliage, the surface of the boughs and trunk, the area below the bark surface, the ground and its vegetation below the tree and, finally, the roots.

These groupings can be broken down further. For instance, there are differences between the top canopy of leaves and the leaves of the lower branches, or beneath the bark of dead or living branches. The creatures that frequent one micro-habitat are not usually found in another.

Opposite page: A tree, which we passed without thought in our youth, will still be standing there, relatively unchanged, when we pass by again in old age – but every year, for hundreds of years, it supports a great, complex community of inter-related life, all of which is dependent on the oak tree in one way or another.

Top: Within the hierarchy, size usually counts for a lot but this bush-cricket should not wait around or it might be attacked from below. The spider's web is strong enough to take the cricket's weight but not strong enough to hold him prisoner without the spider's paralysing bite.

Above: As the leaves open in early May, 'looper' caterpillars, or 'inchworms', hatch and begin feeding in the canopy of the oak. Silken lifelines enable the leaf caterpillars to return to the canopy if dislodged, to make a temporary escape from marauding birds, or finally, to lower themselves to the ground to pupate. Some species, however, pupate in the foliage. All these caterpillars will provide food for the families of young birds that have also just hatched – this is a further vital synchronizing of events. The photograph here shows the mottled umber moth caterpillar.

Above right: It is no accident that throughout the woodland, on stems, stalks and twigs, hoards of baby caterpillars hatch from rows of eggs at exactly the same time as the tender new leaves unfold. If the two events did not coincide it would cause disastrous ripples throughout the woodland community that would affect many forms of life.

Right: The ground below the tree has different conditions, dangers and advantages. This habitat also has its own populations. Top predators of the insect world there are the several kinds of ground beetle. This is Carabus granulatus who likes rather marshy ground.

We may be justified in thinking that the pattern of life in the tree is a complicated, chaotic mini-jungle where few rules seem to apply. However, this would be a misleading over-simplification and no more true of the tree than of the woodland or the jungle.

Over millions of years, natural selection (survival of those best adapted to suit the conditions) has worked on a continuous trial and error basis and has evolved a balanced system. The trees and their leaves do not grow haphazardly: a twig is only destined to become a branch if it can grow out into a patch of light. Its eventual shape will be determined by that changing area of light. In fact, if we look up at the canopy, not only will we see that the branches and twigs spread out and fit into the total space both vertically and horizontally, but, if we look more closely, we will note that each individual leaf slots into a mosaic where there is very little overlapping in relation to the light above.

The animal life of the wood and of the tree adjusts itself to a similar mosaic pattern: direct competition, which is mutually disadvantageous and wasteful, is avoided. Even those creatures that are similar and live in the same habitat feed on slightly different foods or feed at different times or in different ways. Many types of caterpillars will chew away at the tissue of the leaves; possibly one species will lay their eggs sooner or later than another.

Aphids and froghoppers and other plant bugs will pierce the stalks and veins of the leaves and suck the sap. Creatures such as bees, many types of fly, moths and butterflies will feed on the nectar and pollen which tree flowers provide, while weevils and other creatures feed on the fruit or seeds.

All these creatures are feeding on the vegetation but in different ways; this becomes obvious when one considers their mouth parts. Caterpillars, wasps and beetles have cutting, biting or chewing jaws. Plant bugs have dagger-like piercing tubes; butterflies have long coiled tubes which can probe deep into flowers; and many flies have sponge-like sucker pads. Weevils have boring mouth parts.

Predators also avoid conflict between each other by either catching their food in a different way or at a different time or place, or by specializing and becoming dependent on one species as prey – as the many kinds of ichneumon wasps are parasitic, each one on a different species of insect.

The expression 'biological niche' is used to describe the position that each creature occupies in relation to others in the same community: a position that is determined by its size, by its choice of food, by the way it obtains that food and by the adaptations that enable it to do so. Each creature has its own niche in the overall pattern. Such an arrangement avoids unnecessary and wasteful competition.

Opposite page: Hoverflies, when adult, feed on pollen and nectar, but their larvae are voracious predators upon aphids.

Top: The large emerald moth is one of the few moths to overwinter as a caterpillar. Most caterpillars hatch out of eggs in the spring and early summer. Hatching in late summer, the emerald moth caterpillar attaches itself to the end of a twig as winter approaches and, when it is well camouflaged, it waits for the spring foliage to open. It pupates in a silk cocoon among the dead leaves lying on the ground. The moth emerges in June – the following year.

Above: The tawny mining bee, unlike most other bees, is solitary – it does not live in a nest or colony. It deserves the name because the female digs a vertical shaft, 10–25 cm (4–10 in) deep and lays her eggs in side chambers which are filled with honey and pollen. The hole is often conspicuous as an inch high 'volcano' of fine, freshly excavated sand or soil.

Top right: The chewing jaws of a dragonfly enable 'quick snacks' in the form of gnats, aphids, craneflies and other insects to be captured and consumed. It forms its six legs into an ensnaring 'basket' to capture and consume its prey while in flight, dropping the unwanted portions.

Above right: The weevils are highly specialized. The mouthparts on the end of the long snout can 'drill' deep into the fruits, nuts and seeds upon which the larvae feed. After 'drilling' the hole the weevil reverses itself and lays an egg in the opening. The photograph shows one of the largest, the oak weevil, just about 1 cm (0·39 in) in length.

Centre right: Very noticeable is this small white crab spider, but it would not be so conspicuous in a completely white flower. However, by waiting motionless, it has succeeded in catching a butterfly that is even larger than itself.

Bottom right: One look at the expression on the face of the lacewing with its beaked mouthparts tells us quite clearly that it is a carnivore. Its larva is even more ferocious and feeds particularly on aphids which suck the sap of leaves.

The leaf canopy Most noticeable and, perhaps, numerous in the tree will be the creatures inhabiting the leaf canopy. They will vary from 'leaf miners' – the flat larvae of small moths or flies – that burrow between the top surface and lower surface of a leaf, to beetles like the Inquisitor beetle, which, although it is a member of the ground beetle family, climbs about the foliage at night feeding on caterpillars. These caterpillars will be the larvae of various small moths and sawflies. Their life cycles will vary – some will hatch from eggs laid last summer; other species will pass the winter as pupae; some will survive as larvae, while a few will over-winter as adults. Some such as the oak roller moth caterpillar can be found in the tube of a rolled-up leaf where they will pupate (turn into a chrysalis). Others will 'migrate' to the ground before changing to a pupa. Some caterpillars form silken cocoons or tents in which they are relatively safe. They have an instinct to move towards the light when hungry, leaving the silk tent and moving up the twigs to the tips. When no longer hungry, they seek to escape from light and so find the tent again where they can rest in safety. There will be many different creatures who form the 'grazing population' of vegetarians apart from the caterpillar.

Among the smallest will be the various aphids. There will be leaf-hoppers, plant bugs or capsids, of which there are over 1,600 species in Britain alone, and the shield bugs, most of which are plant-eaters. These creatures, like the caterpillars, are often present in thousands on each tree, so that by the end of the summer there is hardly a leaf that has not been affected. But they will be under constant attack from the carnivorous larvae of some sawflies, snakeflies, scorpion flies, lacewings, various beetles and hover-flies. Most of these larvae will also be predators when in their adult stage. They will be joined by other adult invertebrates; the many spiders and the common wasp and, at night, some of the longhorned grasshoppers or bush-crickets. In the air space around the tree, winged predators, such as robber-flies, hoverflies and the various species of dragonflies will be hunting. Other winged predators will be many species of birds: tits, robins, wrens and many warblers will feed on the insects, especially caterpillars which are the main source of food for their broods of young. When the leaf-eating population is high, predators in the form of house sparrows and starlings will fly considerable distances from urban areas to woods to collect caterpillars for their young.

Above left: The communal web of a family of lackey moth caterpillars, decorated with the empty skins that the young caterpillars have already shed. One has returned to have a look around. The caterpillars of the lackey moth and other caterpillars that form 'tents', sometimes enveloping whole trees, are a very serious threat to orchards and forests, especially in North America.

Above right: 'Leaf-miners' are the larvae of moths and flies. Here on bramble leaves, three or four larvae of a small moth have eaten their pattern. The egg was laid in the leaf at the narrow end of the squiggle. The larva that hatched from the egg began eating and as it ate it grew. Thus, the tunnel became wider and wider until the larva was ready to pupate. Hold the leaf up to the light to see if the 'miner' is still in residence. It will be pale in colour and very flat.

Left: The speckled bush-cricket cannot fly and is usually found in the lower foliage and ground vegetation. Female bush-crickets have a massive egg laying organ, or ovipositor, which slits the leaf stems and deposits the eggs inside.

Top: During the fourteen days since these two young blue tits left their egg shells, thousands of caterpillars and other insects will have provided the means of such a rapid growth rate. That there are birds feeding their young at the same time as there are caterpillars swarming in the trees is a major factor in maintaining the balance of life in the wood.

Above near right: A delicate young nymph of the oak bush-cricket – a more apt name than 'long-horned grasshopper', as these creatures were once called. Capable of weak flight and feeding on small creatures among the foliage, the female lays her eggs in cracks in the bark. The young nymphs hatch out in early summer.

Above far right: One of the many capsid bugs, most of which are plant eaters with piercing and sucking mouthparts forming a long sharp 'beak' which is folded back beneath the head. There are thousands of species, the largest group of which includes cicadas. Some kinds are carnivorous, feeding on other insects.

Centre near right: Most of the shield bugs are plant eaters but this species is a predator feeding on caterpillars. Shield bugs, so named because of their shape, are unusual in that they protect their eggs and young larvae. Shield bugs, are called 'stink-bugs' in America because they have 'stink glands' which they use for defence.

Centre far right: Among the more common predators is the scorpion fly – so called because the male has a curved grasping organ used in mating at the rear end of the abdomen which resembles the scorpion's 'tail'. Prior to mating the male places a globule of spit before the female, and, while she is distracted and feeding upon this bait, the male seizes her abdomen and mates with her. As in many insects, it is the larva that feeds so ferociously on aphids.

Bottom right: Aphids – such as greenfly and blackfly – can reproduce pathenogenetically; that is, by females fertile from birth without the need of sexual fertilization. This can continue for several generations during the summer before a few males are produced. The young are born in alternate generations of wingless and winged individuals. As each female gives birth to young several times a day, the rapidly increasing population of aphids is able to disperse through the winged generations.

Trunk and branches Most of the creatures living on the surface of the boughs and trunk will be 'resting'. The larvae of many of the leaf eaters will crawl into cracks and crevices to pupate, or adult females may deposit their eggs there, sometimes in a silken cocoon. Also resting or hiding during the daytime will be some of the nocturnal hunters who, when darkness comes, can move out along the twigs into the leaf canopy, safe from the birds who might eat them in the daytime.

There is, of course, a bird that specializes in searching the bark of the trunk and boughs for eggs, larvae, pupae or insects. This is the tree creeper, a tiny bird that has a long curved beak suited for probing into cracks and corners. Starting near the base of a tree trunk, it jerkily climbs to the boughs searching all the time. The nuthatch and the tit family are also birds that scrutinize the bark for food but they, with the warblers and others, also hunt through the leaves and twigs and are perhaps the major predators of the leaf canopy.

Woodpeckers are also highly adapted to a life of obtaining their food from the bark of trees, but they can hunt beneath the bark – down into the wood.

The creatures that live and feed under the bark and in the wood are mostly the larvae of beetles and the great woodwasp. One group of beetles – closely related to weevils – is particularly notorious. These are the bark beetles who make the patterns seen on the inside surface of dead bark. The pattern is made by the female beetle boring the egglaying chamber, from which the feeding channels of the larvae radiate, between the bark and the wood. The patterns vary according to the particular species of beetle, of which the most common are the ash bark and large elm bark beetle. The elm bark beetle carries the fungus infection which has killed so many elm trees – the Dutch elm disease.

Several larger beetles bore deeply into trees. By far the largest is the great stag beetle, males of which can be almost 7·5 cm (3 in) in length. The larvae of such beetles, usually feeding on dead or rotting wood, need three or four years to grow to their full size of over 6 cm (2½ in) because large quantities of dead wood must be eaten to acquire sufficient nutriment. The furniture beetle, the powder post beetle and the death watch beetle, which are sometimes responsible for a great deal of damage in our homes and buildings, also occur in more natural conditions in trees. The famous tapping of the death watch is a signal to attract a member of the opposite sex rather than an ominous warning to the human occupants of the building.

The larvae or caterpillars of certain moths also feed in the wood of trees. The leopard moth caterpillar more usually feeds in the wood of the branches whereas the goat moth – so called because the caterpillar gives off a smell resembling that of the 'billy' goat – bores in solid wood and eventually produces a hole into which it is possible to insert a finger. This is often revealed by the debris below.

Left: Behind the loose bark of dead wood many predators rest or wait for unsuspecting prey. The spiders spread tunnel traps, with inviting silk carpets at the entrance, behind which they wait patiently. Not all webs are sticky, some are trip threads which entangle victims. The tiny jumping spiders, often found on tree trunks, build no webs at all but have good eyesight and capture their prey with a powerful leap. Most spiders have eight eyes arranged in various patterns – such arrangements are often an aid to identification. This is just one of the many discoveries you can make.

Above: A creature that frightens many human beings is the great wood wasp, or great horntail. However, it is really quite harmless. Possessing a very long saw-toothed ovipositor, the female can drill through the bark and solid wood of conifers to lay her eggs. The larvae bore deeper into the wood as they feed. Usually three years pass before they have eaten enough to pupate and later they emerge through the bark as wood wasps. The larvae are the favourite victims of a large ichneumon wasp which drills through the bark to lay its egg by the body of a selected larva.

Top: Of all the caterpillars to be found crawling on the bark of oak trees, that of the pale tussock moth must be the most beautiful. Once common in the hop fields, before the days of chemical sprays, it was called the 'hopdog'. The moth is drab compared to the caterpillar, being mottled in shades of grey. The hairs of the caterpillar can cause irritation and blisters on sensitive skins. Hairy caterpillars are generally avoided by predatory birds.

Above right: The brilliant cardinal beetle, so often seen in the summer on flowers and other herbage, has spent its larval 'childhood' feeding in the rotting wood of dead timber and stumps. The adult beetle's fine red coat, hence its name, is composed of a powder of red scales on its wingcases, which are rather like the scales on a butterfly's wing.

Centre near right: The adult stag beetle, like many insects, will require only enough food to enable it to survive to breed – in this case, a little nectar taken from flowers. The great 'antlers' of the male beetle are quite harmless and are used to threaten enemies and other males, and to position and hold the female during mating. The female, on the other hand, although without the

great pincers of the male, can inflict a painful nip.

Centre far right: Largest among the wood borers are the stag beetle larvae, usually feeding on dead apple or oak wood. The adult beetles emerge in June after three to four years of eating rotting wood, and spend a further three or four weeks experiencing the joys and responsibilities of adult life before laying the eggs that will start the life cycle once again.

Bottom near right: This 'rhinoceros' beetle is 15 mm (0·59 in) long. In early July it emerges from the dead wood of beech trees, in which it has lived as a larva and pupa. Unlike the stag beetle, to which this beetle is closely related, the horn-like projections on the head and thorax seem to be useful in giving the head a 'scoop' shape – this is an advantage for the beetle when tunnelling in wood.

Bottom far right: This photograph shows the remarkable pattern created by the elm bark beetle on the underside of the bark. The larger central chamber is used for mating by some species of bark beetle. Notches are made in the sides of the main gallery into which eggs are laid. The side galleries increase in width as the larvae grow.

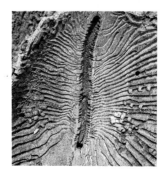

Left: The ground and the vegetation below the tree are affected
by the tree and, in turn, influence
life in the tree itself. Plant or
shrub growth will vary according to the species of tree above.
Wavy hair grass gets sufficient
sunlight to grow on the poor
acid soil beneath this spreading
beech tree.

Above: The plant material that
falls to the ground rots away
continuously. Rotting fruit provides food for many insects.
Here, honey bees have joined a
common wasp, green bottle flies
and fruit flies to imbibe the
sweet fermenting juices of the
pear. Beware, a drunken wasp is
quite capable of stinging.

The ground beneath the tree This is an important habitat for many creatures and is part of the
biological cycle in which the tree takes part. What
the tree produces in branches, twigs, leaves and
seeds eventually reaches the ground and, except for
the seeds, begins to rot. The process is the beginning
of another complex pattern of inter-dependent life,
as important as the one that begins in the tree-tops
with the aphids sucking the sap of the new growth.

The decomposition of the vegetable material
involves bacteria and fungi, and it is this most basic
level of decaying and living matter that provides
food for the minute insects (less than 5 mm [0·19 in])
called springtails, and also the mites that infest the
woodland floor and begin the process of breaking
down the leaf litter into soil.

Feeding on the springtails and mites will be a
host of small creatures, from centipedes and harvestmen to the larger carnivores such as ground beetles.
Snails and slugs are also at work at this level, as
earthworms. A further link with the communities in
the tree above is the number of larvae of various
kinds that will drop or make their way down to the
ground in order to over-winter as pupae in the soil
beneath the tree.

Predatory upon this pyramid of life at ground
level will be the birds that feed in the lower layer of
the wood: for example, the thrushes, blackbirds,
dunnocks, robins and wrens. The invertebrates of
the soil form a very large and important part of the
diet of other animals such as shrews, mice and voles,
and even such larger mammals as the fox and badger.

*Above: The sawflies are an important group of insects, not true flies but related to the bees, wasps and ants (*Hymenoptera*), having two pairs of wings. They are easily distinguished by their thick bodies – they do not have a 'wasp-waist'. Many species of sawflies will be found in the ground vegetation; each lays its egg in a particular way and on a different plant. The larvae of sawflies are rather like small caterpillars but, unlike caterpillars, they have six or more pairs of abdominal legs at the rear end of the body.*

Centre near right: The violet ground beetle and its relatives are flightless and are some of the largest insect predators. They are common nocturnal hunters in the debris of the forest floor. During the day they can be found resting under bark and logs. The larvae are equally ferocious hunters in the soil litter. If molested, most ground beetles can squirt an unpleasant, acrid brown fluid at their attacker.

Centre far right: Nearer the ground in a patch of dead nettles a tiny spider waits, ready for any insect that visits the flower. It

does not build a web or hunt and chase its prey, but remains perfectly still until it finally pounces on its unsuspecting prey. If it moves at all it may well move sideways – this movement, together with its long front legs, accounts for its name – crab spider. There are several different species of crab spiders, many of whom wait in flowers for their prey – often their colouring is white, yellow or pink to match the flower. Crab spiders have some ability to camouflage themselves by changing their colouring.

Below right: The great green bush-cricket (or grasshopper) is largely carnivorous and feeds on other insects. It frequents the lower vegetation on and below the tree – the branches, bushes and brambles. Here, in August, the female lays her eggs deep in the soil, where they remain until they hatch out the following June. The adults soon die as the frosts of winter set in. Bush-crickets 'sing' by rubbing their forelegs together – most species do this at night, but the great green species will sometimes even break into 'song' during the daytime.

Ichneumon and gall wasps are two groups of insects that are rather exceptional in the pattern we have considered. The ichneumon wasps, of which there are at least 1,200 species in Britain alone, break the pattern of little creatures being eaten by bigger creatures who are themselves eaten by even larger predators. The ichneumon wasps are parasitic in highly specialized ways on different species of insects, which they attack in the larval stage by laying their egg or eggs inside the body. Obviously, if they are to continue feeding on the larva, the ichneumon larva must be considerably smaller to avoid killing its host until it is itself nearly full grown. The largest of the common ichneumon wasps (*Ophion luteus*) attacks several related species of moth caterpillars, including the startling caterpillar of the sycamore moth and that of the goat moth. After the moth caterpillar has spun its cocoon, which is virtually the last thing it does before it finally dies, the ichneumon larva emerges through the caterpillar's skin and pupates beside it.

Sometimes the process becomes very complex, when one of an even smaller group of wasps – the chalcid wasps – lays its egg parasitically in the body of the ichneumon parasite! The chalcids are a numerous group of minute members of the wasp

Above: Ophion luteus *is one of the largest ichneumons. It frequently flies into lighted houses and, as it can deliver quite a painful sting, should be treated with respect. The female, unlike most ichneumons, does not have a long ovipositor. She lays her eggs in the caterpillars of the sycamore moth, the puss moth and one or two others and the larva emerges through the caterpillar's skin.*

Below: There are many different kinds of ichneumon wasp; most are parasites in their larval stage on larvae of different insects, especially butterflies and moths. Some small ones are parasites on other ichneumons. Ichneumons are usually easy to recognize – with narrow waists, constantly moving antennae, and long ovipositors. We do not know, even now, how they detect their prey.

family. Many of them are brilliant metallic colours, often green, and generally under 3 mm ($\frac{1}{8}$ in) in length. Most of them are parasitic and live on other insects. One group of chalcids, called fairy-flies, are exceedingly small – a third of a millimetre in length. They need to be tiny for they lay their eggs inside the eggs of small bugs and plant lice.

Closely resembling the chalcids is another group of small members of the *Hymenoptera* – the gall wasps. The word 'hymenoptera' means membranous wings. All the families in the order *Hymenoptera*, which includes the bees, wasps and ants, have two pairs of wings which are sometimes virtually hooked together and look like one pair. The gall wasps are the second exceptional group, breaking the pattern in another way. They live within buds and leaves, and fall to the ground with them to continue the next stage of their lives, in some cases the next generation, in another micro-habitat – the leaf litter on the ground. These are the insects that rather mysteriously cause galls to grow on many plants and trees.

Above: This large white butterfly has just emerged from the chrysalis case. It was lucky – a surprisingly high proportion are parasitized by a small braconid wasp while they are still caterpillars, in which case only braconids come out of the pupal case.

Below: Beech leaves which have been galled by a midge. The egg is laid under the upper surface in the spring. As the gall grows, the larva feeds within the central chamber in the gall. The gall drops off when the leaves fall, and the midge emerges safely in the spring.

Right: The sycamore moth caterpillar is brilliantly coloured – the

black and white spots on its back 'wink' as it moves. Being hairy, with conspicuous colouring, it presumably has little to fear from birds. The moth is clothed in a disappointing uniform grey.

Below: The spectacular, red, hairy robin's pin-cushion gall which grows commonly on wild roses and is also caused by a gall wasp, Diplolepis rosae, is pictured here. Many eggs are laid in a bud in the spring; the larvae have finished feeding by the winter when they pupate, and then emerge as adults in the following May. If the larvae are collected in late winter, the gall wasps may be bred in glass jars.

Galls are strange cancerous growths on plants that are caused by insects (often tiny wasps). In the gall, the young insects can feed and grow in safety. We really know little about how they are caused. Probably when the adult insect lays its egg, it affects the plant's cells chemically, stimulating them to grow rapidly and abnormally. Each insect causes a very special form of growth on the plant – a ball, swelling, projection, bud or seed-like growth – which is particular to that species of insect only. Galls occur on many plants other than trees, (for instance, thistles) but of the trees, the oak is the one which is most affected by a great variety of galls. There are at least twenty common ones.

Most galls have a very strange double generation life-story. For instance, from the galls that provide a safe refuge over the winter emerge females that are capable of laying fertile eggs without the need of a male to fertilize them. This is called uni-sexual or parthenogenetic generation. These eggs cause galls which are completely different from the ones in which the females spent the winter. These second galls contain females *and* males (bi-sexual generation). Both sexes emerge during the summer and mate after which the female lays the eggs which form the autumn/winter galls containing only the fertile females. The year's cycle is then complete; two generations, one of females only, each causing the growth of a different form of gall, both galls being peculiar to that species of gall wasp.

Once again, however, the story is even more complicated. A gall such as the oak marble gall, although caused by a minute gall wasp, frequently becomes a community itself. Not only is the tiny gall wasp often parasitized by small chalcid wasps, but the chalcids may be parasitized by even smaller hyperparasites (parasites of parasites) – the braconid wasps. But there is more – other gall-wasps, cuckoo-like, lay eggs in the gall and their larvae become uninvited lodgers as do the larvae of some flies and small moths who have laid their eggs in the gall. All of these, too, can be attacked by their own parasite chalcids and braconids.

There are yet further dangers from predator larvae who work their way through the gall, devouring any other larvae they may come across. All these complicated events can take place in a 25 mm (0·98 in) marble gall or a spongy 40 mm (1·57 in) oak apple gall. Community life is even more complex in the 'robin's pin-cushion' gall which is found on wild roses.

It is not surprising that the life-cycles of many gall wasps have been unravelled only in recent decades and some of this is still in doubt, while the intricacies of life in the larger gall lodging houses have been very incompletely studied.

Top: These oak apple galls are rosy and spongy at first but become hard later.

Opposite top: These root galls are growing on a young oak. Here the larvae will pass the winter underground.

Above: These currant galls are shown on young foliage: they are often found on male catkins.

Below: A marble gall cut open showing the pupa of a gall wasp. When the change is complete, the adult will bore its way out.

Oak Galls

All these galls are from the oak tree. Those on the left page are the bi-sexual spring and early summer generations; those on the right are the uni-sexual autumn and winter generations. The lists below name five common gall wasps and show their bi-sexual and uni-sexual generation pairings. Photographs of two pairs are shown at the top of both pages.

Bi-sexual	**Uni-sexual**
(early summer generation)	*(autumn generation)*
Oak apple gall	Root gall
Currant gall *(catkin and leaf)*	Common spangle gall
Marble gall	*Uncertain**
Violet egg gall *(bud)*	Cherry gall
Blister gall *(leaf)*	Silk button spangle gall

*It is asserted that the uni-sexual generation of the marble gall forms on the turkey oak, but this is questionable and further investigation is required.

Above: The larvae of these common spangle galls will emerge as fertile females in the spring.

Centre right: These silk button galls are another type of spangle gall. They are winter galls from which only females will emerge.

Below right: These cherry galls are shown on a leaf in November. Like spangle galls, they fall to the ground with the leaf.

Below left: This cherry gall has been cut open revealing the gall wasp.

Observation in the field

If you are intrigued by the mini-worlds that exist in the woodland turn a leaf or two and take a look at the immense variety of life on the underside.

Once you have done that you will wish to see more. A hand lens (5 ×, 8 × or 10 × is sufficient) is an essential and inexpensive piece of equipment. It is obtainable from most opticians or shops dealing in optical equipment. Hold the lens close to the eye, resting your hand on your cheek, and move the object you wish to look at *up towards the lens* until it is in focus.

A small glass or plastic tube of the type used for pills will make a suitable specimen container. The diameter should be no more than 20 mm or the insect may be out of focus when you use your lens.

A useful piece of additional equipment is a square metre of white cloth or plastic. If this is held or spread beneath a low branch and then the branch is given a sharp blow you will be surprised at the collection of creatures you now have to examine.

You will have difficulty if you try to identify everything – be content with deciding upon the group to which the creature belongs. You then know more about it and its way of life and an examination of its mouth parts and other features will provide you with still more information.

Top: The striking garden tiger moth emerges from the chrysalis in late July and frequently flies towards lights. Distinctive colouring indicates that the moth is distasteful to predators.

Above: The caterpillar of the garden tiger moth is widely known as the 'woolly bear' or 'hairy jack' and is usually found in June. Eggs are laid in late July or early August and the young caterpillar hibernates through the winter and reappears to continue feeding in the spring.

Below: The world of aphids and ants can best be watched on the plant as the ants are constantly moving up and down, taking the honey-dew. However, in order to watch the rapid increase of aphids or the many other predators such as the 'lady-bird' beetle larva – shown here – or the hoverfly larvae, it is easy to take a sprig of thistle or nettle or whatever you find the creatures feeding upon and place it in water. The sprig will be a self-supporting community for some days.

Some groups of insects are easy to establish and identify – for example, caterpillars, beetles, moths and butterflies, other flying insects (with clear wings), spiders and finally the miscellaneous crawlers.

These groups can then be split up into smaller divisions. For instance, how many true legs and how many sucker legs do the caterpillars have? Where are they positioned? The beetles will vary in their general shape and the relative proportions of the head, thorax and abdomen; look at the legs, the antennae and the mouth parts. The clear-winged flying insects will be numerous; those with two wings will be flies; four wings signify that they are bees or wasps including the ichneumons and others. Look closely, the wings may be 'hooked' together as one. Among the miscellaneous will be various larvae, plant bugs, aphids and weevils (which are beetles) – now a book will help.

Observation at home

A large clear jar with a lid is suitable for keeping insects for brief observation. Place a leafy twig inside the jar.

If you wish to keep them long then replace the lid with an old piece of nylon stocking held with an elastic band. Stand the leafy twig in a small jar of water and plug some cotton wool around the stem of the twig – this will prevent the creatures falling in and drowning. Do not worry if the cotton wool becomes damp – sprinkle a *little* sugar or put a tiny smear of honey on it. This will provide food for the captives.

Do not be surprised if some insects are eaten by others – that would have happened on the tree anyway.

A more elaborate cage can be made with a round sweet or biscuit tin and a sheet of clear acetate joined with sellotape. Drill some holes in the lid and glue some nylon stocking over them.

Provide an inch or two of loose soil in the bottom of the tin for pupating caterpillars. Pupation in late summer or autumn signifies that the insect will not emerge until the spring, in which case leave the container in a cool place and keep the soil fairly moist.

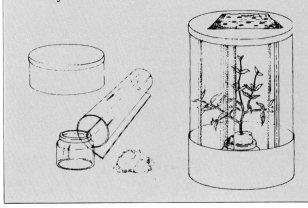

Top right: Two generations of the small tortoiseshell butterfly are produced each year. The butterfly hibernates, then re-appears in the spring and lays eggs which become caterpillars in June. By July the new butter-flies emerge and lay another batch of eggs from which more butterflies evolve in September. These tortoiseshells hibernate and, in turn, start the first brood the following year.

Centre right: Caterpillars of the small tortoiseshell butterfly that are found in June on stinging nettles, will grow rapidly and pupate (turn into a pupa, or chrysalis) on stalks, hanging from self-produced pads of silk.

Bottom right: The pupa, or chrysalis, will be a light yellow-ish green at first and will darken to a very dark grey or brown just before the butterfly emerges.

Habitats and Survival

What did house sparrows do before man built houses for them? This is not such a strange question, for they were once probably quie uncommon and existed only in certain local areas, perhaps restricted to cliffs, until man changed things. Such a history applies to much that is common and familiar to us.

Man has been increasingly changing the world for 5,000 years. When we glibly say, 'leave things to Nature', 'go back to Nature' or 'let Nature take its course', we mean that man should stop manipulating the natural environment temporarily, for it would take thousands of years for the effects of man's presence to disappear into insignificance.

But there is not one totally 'natural' condition or state of being. A natural environment is in balance, but it is the balance of a tight-rope walker: the rope is continually shaking, whipping and jerking; an equilibrium exists which constantly readjusts itself in counterpoise to changing external and internal influences.

There are surprisingly few places left in the world which are 'natural' in that they are relatively unaffected by man. The fast-disappearing equatorial rain forests are the first that come to mind, some remote coral islands, the tundra lands, and polar regions, the high deserts (those that have not been created by man) and perhaps the more remote salt marshes on our coasts. Apart from the latter, all are places that are difficult for most of us to reach. A few relics remain nearer to hand, however, isolated and often preserved as national parks or nature reserves – these are often little patches of fen-land, sand-dunes, peat bogs, primordial forest, grassland, heaths and moorland.

In each of these environments some elements of the original communities of plants and animals still exist and we can obtain some idea of how things once were.

What *is* natural around us is the continuous process of reversion 'back to nature', the reassertion of the cyclic natural conditions which existed before the particular man-made change took place. For example, many of the great coniferous forests of North America have been gradually cut down over the last hundred years and, generally, little replanting has occurred. In their place, a scrub forest of trees and other plants has again reasserted itself – some of the fauna have survived, too. The tall, beflowered grasslands of the original prairie now exist only in nature reserves and many of the specialized plains animals live under protection, too.

What happened a century ago in North America – the indiscriminate removal of the tree cover and

Top: A beaver lake in the remnants of what, one hundred years ago, were the great white pine forests of Minnesota and Wisconsin. The great pines have been felled and a cover of aspen, white birch and jack-pines are re-growing. The beaver's lodge is visible in the background of the photograph.

Above centre: An East Anglian salt marsh changing with the coastline – but in much the same natural conditions that have existed for centuries. Now it contains typical plants – sea lavender, sea purslane and sea aster – that have helped create the marsh by consolidating and stabilizing the mud after the initial colonizers.

Above: In heathland, a wet peat-bog with its characteristic plant community of sphagnum moss, bog asphodel, cotton grass and sundew.

the ploughing in of the protective grass mat that held the soil in place – is now happening in South America and in Africa. Nearly a thousand years ago it happened in Britain and Europe, but then it was a more gradual process because man did not have the technical ability to bring about the great and sudden changes that are possible in the twentieth century. As the uplands and lowland woods were cleared of trees, heathers, grasses and plants, that had existed on a small scale between the trees, took over and became dominant in these areas. The peat layers, when examined microscopically, show a sudden increase of pollen from grasses and what are now farm weeds, at a time which coincides with the spread of farming. Early farming methods involved shifting cultivation, clearing woodland, growing crops for a few years and then moving on to a fresh area.

The natural recolonization processes commenced as the early fields were abandoned. A similar course of events followed the decline of sheep grazing for wool. In this way, the once wooded hills were gradually overgrown with the familiar purple heather we see today.

Above: The old prairie, with its deep rich soil that held the rain and was protected by a mat of grasses that grew 2·5 m (8 ft) high, was also covered with a mass of flowers familiar to gardeners in Britain and Europe – sunflowers, rudbeckias, bergamot, golden rod and many others. Today, the original prairie flora is in desperate need of preservation; contour ploughing and alternate strip cultivation is needed to preserve the rich soil from both wind and water erosion. Over-cultivation and the use of insecticides, combined with natural erosion, have endangered the prairie flora.

Top right: The well-known prickly pear, growing in the deserts of Colorado, is a highly specialized plant adapted to meet desert conditions. Capable of withstanding extremes of heat and cold, of storing large amounts of water and with a tough, leathery skin, the prickly pear requires very little water each day to exist.

Near centre right: The brilliant red bunch-berries are part of the typical shade and moisture-loving ground flora that contrive to grow as the woods regenerate themselves. Bunch-berries can be found in the great northern forests of the United States. Much of this woodland flora has survived.

Far centre right: The mountain pansy is a plant found only in upland pastures and grassland. It is found in many parts of Europe, including the British Isles and especially in the Yorkshire dales. It is often referred to as 'shepherd's pansy' or 'yellow violet'. Mountain flora in many places is in need of protection from 'man, the tourist'.

Bottom right: The sundew – an insectivorous plant of the acid bogs – is restricted to this particular habitat and consequently is a very local plant. Here shown in close-up, its leaves are equipped with glandular hairs, each terminating in a sticky globule with which it entraps small flies and digests them. The leaves react when an insect lands.

Man-changed habitats To arrange the land-scape so that it feeds man efficiently, it has been necessary for man to create very strange and un-natural habitats. Vast areas exist where one plant grows predominantly alone, supported by one or two lesser plants, and plagued by a few insects which specialize in feeding on the main plant and which form the prey of one or two specialist predatory insects. The crop plants all make the same demands on the soil and have the same effect upon it. All grow at the same rate, mature simultaneously and become susceptible to the same pest at the same time.

Such simple relationships in an area are very vulnerable to sudden fluctuations. The effects of slight changes are rapidly accumulative – popu-lations of insects will rise and fall very quickly. This will not only affect pest insects but also pollinating insects and predators among the insects which normally have the effect of dampening down the worst surges of pest populations.

So this 'mono-culture', which is what we must practise to produce food efficiently, tends to favour a few dominant species of insects and to reduce the variety and richness of natural life. This dilemma is present in the case of fields sown for hay or silage crops and also in grazing sheep and cattle, where old original pastures have been ploughed and resown. In this way, we lose the variety of plants and animal life and tend to produce an unstable ecological situation.

This reduction of species could be more serious than it appears. There is much more at stake than the aesthetic and amenity loss. What has been called the 'gene-pool' is poorer. The potential for variation within species is the basis of evolution, both for the creation of new varieties which may become new species and also for developing adaptations to meet changing conditions. Not only will the processes of natural change suffer, but the scope for breeding new, improved varieties of plants and animals is also greatly restricted.

The need to use ancient genetic strains in developing improved animal stocks is well known but it also applies to grasses, other crops and to trees. Variation in elm trees is shown by the fact that some are more resistant to 'Dutch elm disease' than others. It is not known why – but natural re-generation of trees from the hedgerows will ensure continued and greater variation and flexibility than replanting with trees from nurseries with a narrower genetic origin; it will also provide a long-term insurance against sudden calamities like the 'Dutch elm disease' which has killed thousands of elms in Britain over the last few years.

It is also necessary in the interests of efficiency to enlarge fields by reducing the numbers of hedgerows but here, too, there are possible long-term dangers to weigh in the balance.

Hedgerows – which, if considered as linear woodland, comprise a larger area than actual wood-land in Britain – are important reservoirs of genetic

Opposite page: A field of wheat will favour one or two specialist pests and their predators. The narrow balance creates control problems especially as, with greater mechanization, fields become bigger.

Above: Old pastures, containing a rich community of plants, are important as reservoirs of genetic variation and for the conservation of plants that are becoming rare.

Above right: Verges and moist corners of marginal land can be important mini-conservation areas. They help to maintain the variety of flora and fauna and enrich the countryside. Planned

cutting of roadside verges or occasional grazing in other places controls rank growth. Buttercups, ragged robin and flowering grasses are part of the beauty of the June countryside.

Right: Removal of hedges exposes land to wind erosion. Crops are often either eroded or buried. Spring winds had this effect on a light Suffolk soil.

Below: Hedgerows support populations of insectivorous birds and animals by providing breeding sites. The song thrush, whose mud-lined nest in a hedge is shown here, has a diet that is 70 per cent animal and 30 per cent vegetable.

variation. The removal of hedges, trees and copses, in some cases, amounts to the removal of shelter for many animals and birds as well as the consequent danger of exposure to wind erosion. There is little evidence of any serious detrimental effects on agriculture.

The loss of wild flowers, attractive insects such as butterflies, song birds, interesting animals and other attractive aspects of the landscape are more serious in the form of severe deterioration in the recreational and amenity use of the countryside.

However, over the last few years, there has been more cause for concern about losses due to the use of herbicides and insecticides.

The food cycle During the last two decades, the effects on vegetation of chemical sprays – both herbicides and pesticides – the use of chemically treated seed and the results of heavy use of chemical fertilizers have been widespread and sometimes serious.

Lack of research means there is little hard evidence to *prove* that chemicals are responsible for the decline in insect and bird populations, but what evidence there is has been sufficiently convincing for governments to declare that there is a potential danger to plants, animals and man.

Lowland areas with a high proportion of arable farm land are now noticeably devoid of butterflies, whereas twenty years ago these insects were common. Areas where cultivation is not so intensive have higher populations of butterflies. This difference can be accounted for partially by mechanization leading to large-scale, tidy farming with fewer 'weedy' corners of marginal land where the food plants of many butterflies grow. Food plants will also have been eliminated by the use of herbicides.

It is unnecessary to emphasize again the close links between the plant-eating pests and their predators, which include insects, birds and animals, all

Above: This male kestrel has just delivered a vole to its nest. When the more harmful pesticide chemicals were in widespread use and the vole had been eating treated seed, the poisons would have started to build up inside the month-old kestrels.

Upper far left: Vegetation was the food of most of the worms, caterpillars and other insects that fed this fledgling song thrush while it grew in the nest. On the day that it left the nest a pair of magpies caught and killed two of the brood of five.

Upper near left: The pheasant that laid these eggs feeds on seeds, berries, vegetation and insects. The magpie found and began to eat the clutch of eggs. An intelligent bird, the magpie will persist until it has had all the eggs. The pheasant must try again elsewhere.

Centre far left: This magpie was careless while hunting on the ground – a fox had approached silently through the vegetation and pounced. The corpse was hidden and heavily marked by the fox's scent: foxes seem to prefer their food 'high'. The magpie has been arranged in the photograph in order to show the characteristic pattern and shape of the wings and tail feathers and the distinctive colouring.

Centre near left: The fox, who will also feed on voles, mice, worms, beetles, blackberries and young pheasants (before they can fly), will have no natural enemy other than the gamekeeper and the farmer – surprisingly, he may do more good than harm to the farmer by killing rabbits and small mammals which damage his crops.

Lower far left: The gamekeeper will protect his hen pheasants sitting on their eggs, and later their growing chicks, by setting snares for the fox. In this bluebell wood, where pheasants are nesting, he has disguised his steel wire noose, staked to the ground, with an arch of twigs set across a narrow but well used path. Unfortunately, such snares are a danger to animals other than foxes, and condemn them to a lingering and extremely unpleasant death. Some of the worst traps are now banned.

Lower near left: Foxes which have been caught by the gamekeeper will be killed and tossed aside. Their bodies, like the roadside corpse of the mole, will first be attacked by maggots, the larvae of flies, then by beetles, until only a few bones remain as evidence of the creature. Notice the spade-like, digging forefoot of the mole shown here in the photograph.

Above: The fawn of the fallow, deer, one hour after birth. The fawn, like the leveret below, is exclusively herbivorous. Both young creatures 'freeze' to simulate death and thus avoid danger and both are camouflaged to assist in concealment and are often left alone by their mothers to lessen the chance of discovery by predators. However, in the case of the fallow deer, predators are only dangerous in the first few days or weeks of life. The natural predators of the deer – the wolf, hyena and, for fawns, the lynx – are no longer found in the wild in Britain. The wolf and the lynx are still present in Northern Europe in small numbers but are largely irrelevant – this is also true of much of North America. The hyena is a native of Africa. Nowadays, the deer's enemy is man.

Below: The young hare, or leveret, active almost from birth, is placed in a separate grassy hollow – 'form' – from its brother by the female hare. The mother hare's policy of not putting all her leverets in one 'basket' is in case there should be predatory foxes about. The hare is exclusively a grazing herbivore (plant-eater) – with several carnivorous enemies who prey upon it, such as foxes and badgers.

of which are affected by the treatment of a crop. A prey species must always have a higher breeding rate than the species that is predatory upon it; thus the pest can quickly return in greater numbers.

Insect-eating birds, such as the skylark, are affected when they eat poisoned insects. Infertility results and the population drops. Birds of prey, like the sparrow hawk, a bird that hunts fast and low along the hedgerows, feed on the smaller insect-eating birds such as the chaffinch and, because these predators live longer, the poisons build up to a high level of concentration. This has been proved by analysis of corpses and infertile eggs. The sparrow hawk became virtually extinct in some areas and the decline in numbers of birds of prey generally was striking. Less noticeable at first was the decline of many small birds whose diet included a large amount of insects – birds such as the chaffinch, treepipit, skylark, yellow-hammer, many common warblers, turtle dove, partridge and even the cuckoo.

By eating chemically treated seeds, poisons accumulate in mice and voles. In turn, the poisons build up in the birds that feed on these animals – the owls and kestrels. The effect, however, was not as devastating as in the case of the sparrow hawk because the small mammals also occur in areas free of chemicals – woodland, rough pasture and motorway verges.

The pattern of the food web is often described as pyramidal. The large numbers at the bottom being basic vegetation eaters, while primary, secondary and even tertiary predators are present in decreasing numbers. In considering one tree, it may well be found to contain thousands of aphids and that these creatures are the main food supply for hoverfly, scorpion fly and laverwing larvae. These will be present at least in hundreds and will be preyed upon by a score of tits and warblers in whose territory the tree is growing. A pair of jays nesting nearby are likely to take a high proportion of young tits and warblers whilst they are nestlings or fledglings. Jays and magpies are ruthlessly persistent when they discover a nest of young birds and will chase young fledglings until fatigue makes them victims.

Because man has removed the larger carnivorous animals and birds such as the wolf, lynx, eagle, peregrine falcon and others, many creatures have lost their natural enemies; for instance the fox, fallow deer and kestrel have no enemies other than man – the ultimate predator. Enemies of the highest predators in a food chain are disease, starvation and themselves. But the food chain completes the circle because the blue-bottle fly larvae begin the process of decomposition, and beetles and bacteria finish it off. The decayed material adds to the nutriment that feeds the vegetation. The cycle is complete and the balance is roughly maintained.

Underwater world To talk of food webs or pyramids is perhaps a complicated way of saying, 'big fish eat little fish'.

Sometimes, in the rather more isolated miniature world of a pond, the complications of the interlocked life cycles and the specializations that different forms of life have undergone appear to be simple and straightforward. But a pond can be even more critically balanced. Changing conditions of sunlight, temperature and water level cause it at times to fluctuate widely. The microscopic plants – algae – flourish until they are too numerous and die from lack of light. Bacteria then multiply until sometimes they, too, pollute the pond with their numbers; minute creatures feed on the bacteria and larger creatures feed on the smaller. Conditions suit one and then another species, each population being adjusted by the 'higher' predator that feeds upon it until a changing balance is achieved and maintained in the pond.

Apart from the dangers outside the pond, such as fishermen, herons, kingfishers, diving ducks, grebes and otters, and the dangers within the water arising from the larger fish, there are predators that, for their size, are as ferocious as any on land. Like the insects of the foliage, it is the larval stage in many creatures that is so voracious. This is to be expected as the adult insect does not grow and needs energy only to pursue its role as a reproducer. The larvae of many beetles, nymphs of dragonflies and the tadpoles of frogs, toads and newts have only one object at this stage of their lives and that is to eat, to grow bigger and quicker before something bigger eats them in turn.

The dragonfly lays its eggs in the pond during the summer and dies at the end of the autumn, but the nymph, as the larva is called, that hatches from the egg will live through the winter frosts safe in the water below the ice. In the case of the larger species of dragonfly, the nymph may live for up to four years before metamorphosis (the change to adult form) occurs.

These nymphs are hunters that are just as stealthy as any lizard or snake. Moving imperceptibly slowly, they creep towards their prey, pausing with great patience until they are within range. Then, suddenly, from beneath the 'chin' a long folding, hinged, 'arm' equipped with a vicious pincer-like claw shoots out, grabs the victim and draws it back to the mouth.

The fierce larva of one of the largest water beetles – *Dytiscus marginalis*, the great diving beetle – is also a ferocious carnivore in its adult form. Like most water beetles, it can emerge from the water, often at night, to fly to another pond. There is sometimes considerable movement by water beetles, as in-

Above: The larva of the great diving beetle is frequently seen 'hanging' from the surface of the water, taking in air through two breathing tubes which are pushed through the surface film. Its body is lighter than water.

Below: A tadpole's-eye-view before the deadly pincer lunges out. This dragonfly nymph has just shed its outer casing. This happens just twelve times while the nymph lives at the bottom of the pond, stream or lake.

dicated by the speed with which beetles appear in freshly filled ponds. The large, curved, piercing jaws of the great diving beetle larva are modified in a peculiar way. At the tip of each pointed jaw a canal opens which leads back to the 'throat'. When the jaws have closed on a victim, digestive juices are pumped down into its body to dissolve the tissues. The resulting 'soup' is sucked back up the canals and down into the larva's gut, until nothing but an empty 'husk' is left of the prey – this is then cast aside. The

Dytiscus larva takes in air by means of two breathing tubes in the tail-end of its body as it hangs from the surface of the water.

Dragonfly nymphs do not breathe air but take up oxygen from the water. Several species of dragonfly have gills in the lower part of the gut, to perform this function. Water is sucked in and out through the anus so that it can pass over the gills. In an emergency, rapid acceleration can be obtained by jet propulsion of water in this way.

Near right, far right, below left and right (group of four pictures): One evening in the late June of the fourth year from the beginning of the life cycle of the dragonfly, the nymph climbs a pond-side reed and pauses; the casing of the creature splits open down the thorax and the dragonfly begins to haul itself out. The white threads showing in these photographs are old linings of the nymph's breathing tubes. Hanging backwards and gathering its strength, it suddenly flicks itself forward and *clings on with its feet so that it can withdraw its abdomen. Now the folded wings are literally pumped up and air taken in to swell the body. Within two or three hours both wings and body-casing will harden – full size must be reached by then – and the first flight for the newly emerged dragonfly will be possible after a further rest. In the early morning sun, the dragonfly will commence its airborne hunting, flitting across the water, its irridescent wings shimmering in the sunshine.*

Defensive behaviour It is easy to see that the 'eagles', 'wolves' and 'tigers' of the insect world are equipped with some terrifying weapons, but can they justly be accused of possessing *offensive* weapons? Certainly they are deadly but they are the tools of their trade – they are used merely to acquire food. Those insects that use weapons for purposes other than capturing and killing their food use them for defensive purposes. Most of the *Hymenoptera*, the bees and wasps, have stings but they are present only in the females or the asexual 'workers' in the social bees and wasps. This is so because the sting is an adaptation of the ovipositor or egg-laying organ. Apart from the queens, who use their stings to kill other young queens, the stings and associated poison glands are used by workers in defence of the hive or nest. The solitary wasps and ichneumons use their stings in different ways. Ichneumons pierce their prey's body with the ovipositor in order to deposit their eggs inside. Solitary wasps have developed the ovipositor as a sting to paralyse their victim which they then store as food for their larvae.

Defensive behaviour takes many forms, for example, in some cases it is speed or flight. Erratic flight is a means of defence for butterflies; insects like grasshoppers and frog-hoppers use speed when jumping. Others remain perfectly still to escape detection, while many spiders feign death.

There are, however, more positive forms of

Above: The beautiful peacock butterfly has very distinctive 'eye' markings which, when the wings are suddenly flicked open, have a startling effect on predators. The bristle-like hairs of the caterpillar also have a deterrent effect on would-be attackers. The undersides of the wings are rather drab and camouflaged.

Below: The magpie moth pictured here, conspicuously marked, tastes unpleasant to its predators. The colours, like those of the larva and the yellow and black striped chrysalis, are 'helpful' recognition colours which, for a predatory bird, are saying 'once tasted, twice shy'. Many insects are brightly coloured so as to deter predators.

Above left: The wood ant can both bite and inject formic acid, which it can also squirt in defence of the nest. It should be left alone if possible. When a few are imprisoned in a small jar for a few minutes the smell of the acid is very strong when the lid is removed.

Upper right: The elephant hawk moth caterpillar gains its name from its likeness to an elephant. The forepart of the caterpillar is swollen and then tapers towards the head. The swollen part is marked with two pairs of eye marks. When disturbed, the caterpillar extends the 'trunk' and thus enlarges the eyes. By waving the trunk to and fro the resemblance to an elephant is quite surprising.

Lower right: The lobster moth

caterpillar is one of the most fantastic of all caterpillars, deriving its name from its resemblance to a lobster. When alarmed, the caterpillar's threatening behaviour is much more like that of a spider. Two pairs of the three pairs of true legs are extremely long and the caterpillar raises the front part of its body and waves the four long legs in the air. At the same time, the enlarged rear section of the body is raised and stiffened to increase the frightening appearance. If this is unsuccessful it can also squirt formic acid at an attacker.

Below: A gravid female oil beetle may contain up to ten thousand eggs. They are necessary because the chances of survival are very slim for an oil beetle larva – only two survive out of every ten thousand eggs laid.

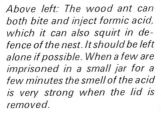

escaping from enemies. Many creatures – beetles, sawfly larvae, some moths and their caterpillars – have an unpleasant taste. In these cases it is an advantage to the species also to have a means of ensuring that the bird or animal that made the attack is quick to recognize the prey species again. This is usually assisted by conspicuous colours, patterns or behaviour. Some beetles and ants can squirt unpleasant liquids or smells at potential attackers which in the case of ants is formic acid and can be squirted more than 15 cm (6 in). Many of these liquids are merely distasteful, but some are irritants. The large oil beetle, together with one or two other beetles, has an irritant in its blood which, on being attacked, oozes from around its joints.

Many of the hairy caterpillars are not only unpleasant to eat because of their hairiness, but the hairs themselves contain an irritant.

Warning colours that are virtually saying 're-member, I am unpleasant', are very similar in function to other markings and colours which are intimidating and threatening. Many of the hawk moth caterpillars wriggle convulsively and twist their coarse and horny skinned bodied when touched. Others, like the lobster moth caterpillar, rear up and threaten their attackers most effectively. Several others, like the elephant hawk moth caterpillar and the peacock butterfly, have markings like eyes which, when moved, have a deterrent effect.

Mimicry The most intriguing kind of defence is what has been called 'mimicry'. One form of mimicry is illustrated where harmless and innocuous insects obtain protection by resembling in colour, shape and markings another insect which is unpleasant or dangerous, such as a wasp. Predators have learned by experience to recognize and avoid the wasp and so mistakenly leave the mimic alone. This method works as long as the wasps are considerably more numerous than the mimics. Were it not so, the wasps themselves would suffer from attack because the birds' experience would be of the harmless insect – the mimic – rather than of a deterrent wasp.

There is another form of mimicry where, for example, it is an advantage for several kinds of wasp to have similar colouring and markings. In these circumstances, the number of attacks needed for the bird to learn to recognize the colours are not repeated for each species of wasp and protection is acquired more quickly and with less loss to the wasp species.

For mimicry to be successful, it is important that both imitator and imitated must occur in the same place at the same time. Most moths are nocturnal but the clearwing moths, which imitate solitary wasps which fly in the daylight, must therefore be diurnal too.

The great migrating butterfly of North America, the monarch or milkweed (as it is called in Britain

Above: Hoverflies are true flies that mimic bees and wasps in colour and markings. There are many different species – 250 in Britain alone. In many species the larva is carnivorous, devouring aphids – one larva in captivity consumed between 800–900 aphids. The adults, however, are vegetarians and feed mainly on nectar.

Below: Another insect that frequents flowers is the spotted longhorn beetle, pictured here, it is also protectively coloured but whether this is a resemblance to wasps or a way of breaking the outline shape of the beetle, using suitable colours for camouflage in flowers, is difficult to say. It is certainly effective as camouflage.

after its food plant), which travels from Mexico to Canada and back, has an unpleasant taste. It is large, conspicuous, and flies slowly when feeding: this is 'warning' behaviour. There is another North American butterfly aptly named the viceroy, the female of which mimics the monarch. Presumably it is an advantage to a species to obtain protection at least for its females who, once successfully mated, will need to spend some time egg laying and, by resembling the monarch, they will gain the advantage of the deterrent effect of its unpleasant taste.

Most mimicry is to deceive the common enemy of both the mimic and the model but there are some remarkable instances in Africa where several species of carnivorous robber-fly so closely resemble the models – each a different species of bee upon which they prey – that the bees themselves are deceived and the robber-flies can kill at will among the bees.

There are many ways in which different species of creatures resemble each other that is not mimicry at all. This is called 'convergent evolution' and it occurs because, living under the same conditions, there is a tendency for those creatures to be successful who adapt themselves to an optimum way of meeting the conditions, whether it is a method of breathing, moving, swimming, catching food or eating it. In other words, given long enough, several unrelated species will find the most successful way of solving the same difficulty and will thus resemble each other in some ways.

Above: The viceroy butterfly of North America. The female profits from being a close mimic of the distasteful monarch butterfly which migrates from Mexico to Canada and back.

Below left: Hardly recognizable as moths, the clearwings resemble solitary wasps and ichneumons. The photograph *shows the red-belted clearwing.*

Below: The brightly coloured longhorn beetle, aptly named the wasp beetle, is a classic example of protective mimicry. The larva feeds by boring into dead stumps and trunks, but the beetle frequents flowers, feeding on nectar. Its resemblance to a wasp gives it protection.

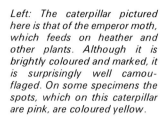

Left: The caterpillar pictured here is that of the emperor moth, which feeds on heather and other plants. Although it is brightly coloured and marked, it is surprisingly well camouflaged. On some specimens the spots, which on this caterpillar are pink, are coloured yellow.

Below left: When at rest, this wasteland grasshopper is beautifully camouflaged, both in colour and by the vertical banding which breaks up the outline of the insect. There are several members of the sub-family Oedipodinae *that 'disappear' when they land after taking flight when disturbed. In flight*

they are conspicuous as the underwing is brightly coloured, in one species light blue and black, in another a delicate red and black. The flash of brilliant colour that suddenly 'switches off' when the grasshopper lands is very confusing, and consequently effective. Wasteland grasshoppers occur in areas of central and southern Europe.

Below right: The colourful patterns on the underside of the red admiral butterfly are mottled and sufficiently distracting to disguise its shape. Notice the butterfly's 'tongue' probing down into the flower to suck up the nectar within.

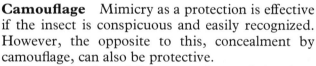

Camouflage Mimicry as a protection is effective if the insect is conspicuous and easily recognized. However, the opposite to this, concealment by camouflage, can also be protective.

Reptiles and amphibians can change their colour and markings to blend with their surroundings. In a sense some insects do this, but as a species rather than as individuals. In different conditions, differing variations of colour or marking will be more or less successful for the survival of the species. The successful variant will then tend to be dominant in the population of the area where the particular conditions apply. The most famous example of this is the peppered moth. Normally a pale grey, mottled moth that is well camouflaged on the lichen-covered trunks of trees, it was noticed in the middle of the nineteenth century that a dark, almost black variety of the moth was increasing and was finally the dominant form in the heavily smoke-polluted in-dustrial towns of the Midlands and north of England. In the woods of the south and west, the pale form continued as the majority but in the industrial areas where it was more conspicuous, it was taken by birds in greater numbers than the dark variety. Whereas in the south and west the dark moths were the more noticeable and so were eliminated. A similar variation has been observed in a species of water boatman, to enable them to escape from enemies or predators. Conversely, a predator may camouflage itself by imitating its surroundings in order to facilitate the capture of its prey – this is the case with some bush-crickets and the well-known praying mantis.

There are two forms of camouflage: colour blending and definite clear markings. The latter is successful because it breaks up the shape and discourages the eye from recognizing it against a varied background. Usually these two 'techniques'

are employed together. Both are particularly noticeable in butterflies at rest. When the two pairs of wings meet over the insect's back, the underside of many species is camouflaged in both markings and colour. The colourful markings on the top of the wings, which are necessary for recognition between the species and the sexes, are then visible in flight.

Concealment sometimes takes quite different forms. The woolly aphid forms a 'cocoon' of waxy material around itself. The frog-hopper nymph creates a soapy froth in which it hides and feeds. The larvae of some lacewing flies decorate the hooks on their backs with the empty 'shells' of the aphids and other creatures which have formed their food, and the gall wasps cause plant cells to grow in an aberrant way to protect their larvae.

Concealment from predators is necessary but it is also essential to advertise your presence to members of the opposite sex of the same species. There are

many fascinating ways in which this is done. Many female moths use their scent to attract the male, sometimes over great distances. The scenting organ of the male emperor moth is the striking pair of feathery antennae. The may-bug or cockchafer beetle has peculiar 'plates' on his antennae; grasshoppers, cicadas and crickets use sound. This may also partly be territorial. Most unusual is the method used by the fireflies and glow-worms, who illuminate parts of their abdomen. They secrete from between plate-like segments two substances which, when in contact with each other, give off light. By opening or closing the segments, the light can be increased or decreased.

There is much that is unknown about how insects perform many of the fascinating functions of their lives – there is even less known about why they do it – but it is happening all the time all around us and it is only necessary to look to see!

Reference books and further reading

For identification in the field or library the following are useful:–

COLLINS GUIDES:–

Butterflies of Britain and Europe	Higgins and Riley
Birds of Britain, Europe & Middle East	Heinzel
Trees of Britain and Europe	Mitchell, Fitter & Parslow
Amphibians and Reptiles of Britain & Europe	Arnold, Burton & Ovenden
Wild Flowers of Britain & N.W. Europe	Blamey, Fitter & Fitter
Birds of Britain & Europe	Paterson, Mountfort & Hollom
Mushrooms & Toadstools	Lange & Hora
Mammals of Britain & Europe	Van den Brink
Animal Tracks and Signs	Bang & Dahlstrom

BLANDFORD:–

Mammals of Britain – Their Tracks, Trails & Signs	Lawrence & Brown
Field and Hedgerow Life	Lyneborg
Woodland Life	Darlington
Plant Galls	Darlington
Oxford Book of Flowerless Plants	Brightman
Oxford Book of Insects	Burton
Oxford Book of Invertebrates	Nichols & Cooke

WARNE – WAYSIDE & WOODLAND SERIES:–

Butterflies of British Isles	South
Moths of British Isles	South
Beetles of British Isles	Linssen
Flies of British Isles	Colyer & Hammond
Bees, Wasps, Ants & Allied Insects of British Isles	Step
Spiders and Allied Orders of British Isles	Savory
Land & Water Bugs of British Isles	Southwood & Leston
Dragonflies of British Isles	Longfield

EBURY & MICHAEL JOSEPH

Concise British Flora	Keble Martin

BLACKWELL

Handbook of British Mammals	Southern

For the younger reader, the following series are very suitable:–

LONGMAN – TOWN & COUNTRY SERIES:–

Autumn Trees	Finch
Growing Trees	Finch
Animals in the Soil	Finch
Pond Animals	Finch

O.U.P. CLUE BOOK SERIES:–

Birds	Allen & Denslow
Flowers	Allen & Denslow
Insects	Allen & Denslow
Trees	Allen & Denslow
Freshwater Animals	Allen & Denslow
Flowerless Plants	Allen & Denslow

Useful background reading:–

COLLINS NEW NATURALIST SERIES includes:–

Britain's Structure and Scenery	Sir Dudley Stamp
Wild Flowers	John Gilmour & Max Walters
Mushrooms and Toadstools	John Ramsbottom
Insect Natural History	A.D. Imms
Trees, Woods and Man	H.L. Edlin
The World of the Soil	Sir E. John Russell
Woodland Birds	Eric Simms

126

Index